G. de La Motte

Piano and Musical Matter

G. de La Motte

Piano and Musical Matter

ISBN/EAN:

Printed in Europe, USA, Canada, Australia, Japan

Cover: Foto ©Thomas Meinert / pixelio.de

More available books at **www.hansebooks.com**

Piano

AND

Musical Matter

2

RESPECTFULLY DEDICATED

TO

M. E. U.

BY'

G. de la Motte.

BOSTON.

WHITE, SMITH & PERRY.

298 and 300 Washington St.

95870

8 043. 26

SECOND EDITION.

THE first edition of a thousand copies was issued on Thursday, October 14th, and to find that within three weeks a second edition is called for, is very gratifying. This second edition gives a favorable opportunity to answer several inquiries made since the publication of this work.

First. The most perfect exercises on scales are, "L'Heure du Matin," by C. Czerny. "L'Etude journalière des Gammes dans tous les tons majeurs et mineurs," by M. Clementi, is shorter, but very good.

Second. As a matter of discipline, it is far better to accustom the pupil to learn the whole of a piece rather than parts of several pieces, such as are found in Instruction Books. Besides, these pieces or rather parts of pieces, having been learned by the older members of a family, are so familiar, that the practising of the younger children is rendered very tedious; moreover, a piece however good, is not best suited to every one; for instance, take the following list of pieces: —

L. van Beethoven,	.	Sonatines 37, 38.
J. Haydn, .	. . .	12 petites pièces.
Mendelssohn,	. . `	. Op. 72.
F. Hiller,	.	. Op. 95.
M. Clementi, .	.	Op. 36.
L. Köhler, .	. . .	. . Op. 133.
J. Schmitt,	. . .	Sonatines.
F. Kuhlau, .	. . .	Op. 55.
J. B. Duvernoy, .	.	. Op. 287.
A. Croisez, .	.	. . Op. 98.
R. Schumann, .	. . .	. . . Op. 68.
F. Kirchner, .	. . . .	. Op. 7, Album leaf.
J. C. W. A. Mozart, .	. .	Rondo in D major, Sonata in F major, Fantasia in D minor.

While one pupil will improve very much by practising Beethoven, another will succeed far better with some other composer; and, finally, any piece desired can be found at the Music Stores.

Third. The intervening practice of such little pieces as a Waltz, a Polka, or La Fille du Régiment, by Le Carpentier, is as improving and as necessary to the pupil as playing out-door is for health; and from this arises the necessity of a first-class teacher for the beginner, — one whose knowledge, care, and tact will discriminate what piece and what studies will be the most improving to the pupil with the same amount of practice.

Fourth. This book will be of great and continuous service; because, after six months or a year, an Instruction Book is generally neglected, while this book, after being used six months by the beginner, will be useful for years afterwards; for, although the first four chapters are exclusively for beginners, the following chapters will give very valuable assistance in interpreting the most difficult compositions of the great masters; and besides, the sketch of the History of Music, the names of the most eminent Musicians, with the places and dates of their birth, etc., render this work valuable to the professional artist as well as to the intellectual mind, whether musical or not.

Fifth. The exercises of the First Chapter *not* being alike for both hands have the great advantage of compelling the beginner to learn the names of the notes in both clefs in the first lessons.

The best manner of practising these exercises is as follows: —

First the names of the notes should be learned, then place both hands in the proper position, one finger on every one of the five notes, and call thus (see page 30): —

"F clef" left hand, third space E. "G clef" right hand, fourth space E.

Lift up the fingers belonging to these notes, and after waiting a moment strike both notes "square" (do not practise one hand alone), replace the hands in the proper position, then call (always the bass first): —

"F clef" left hand, fourth space G. "G clef" right hand, third space C.

Lift up fingers, wait a moment, strike both notes "square," leaving the preceding notes at the same instant. Replace the hands in the proper position, and continue as before.

Part of a line will be sufficient for the first lesson. When this is known and a new lesson given, the old one should be kept in practice.

It will require six months of conscientious study to learn the exercises of the first four chapters as they should be learned, although a short, easy piece may be taken after two or three months' faithful practice, if the teacher thinks it advisable.

It is not the number of exercises played within a half hour that produce the greatest improvement, but the most perfect practising of a few exercises.

Sixth. The following pieces are brilliant and very attractive: —

Johann Nepomuk Hummel,	Op. 120.
K. M. F. E. von Weber,	Op. 79, 62, 72.
Mendelssohn,	Op. 22, 14. 16, 5, 67 No. 34, No. 6493 No 7.
F. Chopin,	Op. 29, 66, 47, 31, 35, 26, 18. Nocturnes, Op. 48, 15, 9.
R. Schumann,	Op. 12, 18, 21 No. 4, 85 No. 10, 15 No. 7.
E. Prudent,	Op. 38, 41.
J. Moscheles,	Op. 71, 54, 82, 38.
F. Hiller,	Op. 97, 55 No. 1, 29 No. 1, 35 No. 1.
S. Heller,	Op. 86, 85 No. 2, 80 No. 2, 89, 97.
F. Liszt,	Soirées musicales No. 9, Cahier 1 No. 3, 2d Rhapsodie Hongroise, Les Patineurs, Galop Chromatique.
S. Thalberg,	Op. 9, 72.
F. Kalkbrenner,	Op. 138, 129.
J. Blumenthal,	Op. 39, 1, 79, 71.
H. Ravina,	Etudes Caractéristiques.

Seventh. The movement or tempo should never be hurried when increasing the tone; neither should it be retarded when decreasing the tone *unless* it is marked on the music.

For want of space, compositions by American Artists are not mentioned here.

CONTENTS.

CONTENTS.

INTRODUCTION.

———

THIS book contains only what is absolutely necessary to be known by every one who wishes to play well on the piano.

He who aspires to become a master of the art must know what it contains, but all that such an one must know is not contained in this book.

Matter about music and a sketch of its early history are given, thinking they may prove interesting even to those who do not play.

A few five-finger exercises and the scales carry the beginner as far as Studies, leaving the teacher to lead the pupil with the following works: —

Duvernoy's Ecole du Mecanisme, opus 120 ;

Czerny's Etudes de la Velocity, op. 299 ;

Stephen Heller's Etudes, op. 47 ;

Czerny's 50 Studies, op. 740 ;

Cramer's Studies ;

Mocheles's Studies ;

S. Heller's Art of Phrasing ;

Mocheles's Etudes Caractéristiques ;

Clementi's Gradus ad Parnassum ;

Chopin's Grandes Etudes ;

Mueller's Le Maître des Maîtres;

or any other order of studies, for the teacher is the one best qualified to judge of the need of the pupil.

No pieces are put in, because an air from Mozart, a sonatine from Beethoven or others, when given to the pupil as a sheet of music, proves to have an influence which it has not otherwise. As for those who already play well, or even very well, the selection of pieces is left to the teacher or to themselves.

It is a great benefit to every one, even to children, to learn both classical and light music, chosen by a judicious teacher : the first cultivates the taste, the second recreates the mind.

* Towards the end of the book there are some Exercises in Scales with accented notes, intended for those who, being able to transpose them in all the keys, can, by changing the accented note, form for themselves new exercises, almost without number.

◄

* See page 84.

A SKETCH OF THE HISTORY OF MUSIC.

THE most ancient musical system of the Greeks was limited to the four strings: " E," " F," " G," and " A." The first and last formed a perfect fourth, and were immovable. Between the first and the second was a diatonic semitone, and this they called a tetrachord, from the Greek τέτρα, four, and χορδή, chord.

Therpander added three strings to the lyre; about the same time a second _{7th Century, B. C.} tetrachord, " B," " C," " D," and " E," was added, forming now a scale of eight strings, which in the sixth century B. C., received the name of " Pythagorean _{6th Century.} lyre " from Pythagoras, who perfected it. New sounds being constantly added, it finally extended to four tetrachords, thus :—

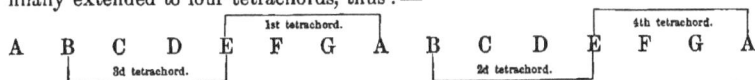

			1st tetrachord.						4th tetrachord.		
A	B	C	D	E	F	G	A	B	C	D	E F G A

3d tetrachord. 2d tetrachord.

In order to make this illustration clearer, the lowest sound is placed first in the scale, as is the present custom; but the Greeks did precisely the opposite, their deepest sound being the upper note, and the highest note being placed lowest in the scale.

There was always a perfect fourth between the two extreme sounds of a tetrachord, and a diatonic semitone between the first two sounds. This is the reason why the Greeks did not begin the division of their musical system at the lowest sound " A," which they called " proslambanomenos," (the added note,) but from the second sound " B," which they called " l'hypate," (fundamental of the fundamentals.)

Two tetrachords united formed the " Heptachord." Two tetrachords divided formed the " Octochord." The " A " in the middle of the scale they called " mesos," (middle note,) and the " B " next to it " paramesos," (next to the middle note.) Between the mesos and the paramesos a new sound, " B flat," was introduced, by which a fifth tetrachord was obtained thus :—

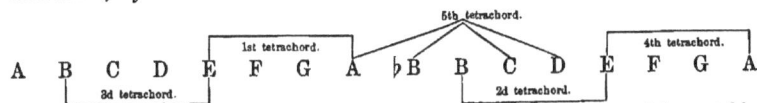

			1st tetrachord.			5th tetrachord.					4th tetrachord.		
A	B	C	D	E	F	G	A	♭B	B	C	D	E F G A

3d tetrachord. 2d tetrachord.

This tetrachordal system, which the Greeks called their great and immutable system, formed the base of the theory of music as late as the eleventh century A. D.

At first there were but three modes, namely: the " Dorian," the " Phrygian," and the " Lydian;" then two more were added— the " Ionian," and the " Æolian." The Greeks used the words " mode," " tone," or " chant " to express the value of the notes. By the value of the notes they understood both their relative and real value.

By the relative value of the notes they meant the interval between them.

The real value of the notes was their length of duration or true value.

Each mode, tone, or chant, began on a given note, ended on a given note, and had its semitones in a given place.

In the fifth and fourth centuries B. C. the scale had two octaves and thirteen modes; but finally the modes were increased to the number of fifteen.

We shall merely give the

NAMES OF THE FIFTEEN MODES OF THE GREEKS:

* Hyper-Lydian.
* Hyper-Æolian.
  Hyper-Phrygian.
* Hyper-Iastian or Hyper-Ionian.
  Hyper-Dorian or (*a*) Mixo-Lydian.
  Lydian.
* Æolian or (*a*) Grave-Lydian.
(*a*) Phrygian.
* Iastian or Ionian.
(*a*) Dorian or (*p*) Hypo-Mixo-Lydian.
(*p*) Hypo-Lydian (grave.)
* Hypo-Æolian.
(*p*) Hypo-Phrygian.
* Hypo-Iastian or Hypo-Ionian.
(*p*) Hypo-Dorian.

The modes marked thus: * were suppressed in the third century B. C.

(*a*) means "authentic," that is, principal mode.

(*p*) means "plagal," that is, derived from an authentic mode.

The early Christians naturally made use of the musical system known in their time.

4th Century, A. D. St. Ambrose, Archbishop of Milan, limited church music to four modes, namely :

The Dorian,
The Phrygian,
The Grave Lydian,
The Mixo-Lydian.

These are the four "authentic" modes; they begin and end on the key-note.

6th Century. Pope St. Gregory the Great added four modes to those of St. Ambrose, namely :

The Hypo-Dorian,
The Hypo-Phrygian,
The Hypo-Lydian (grave,)
The Hypo-Mixo-Lydian.

These are the four "plagal" modes. Each plagal mode begins on the fourth note below the key-note of the authentic mode from which it is derived, and ends on the key-note of that same authentic mode, thus : —

Authentic modes.   Plagal modes.

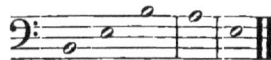

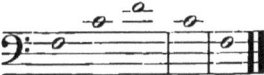

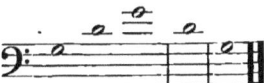

These eight modes are the eight keys, tones, or chants, composing the Gregorian _{Gregorian or Plain Chant} or Plain Chant.

In the authentic modes, the dominant is the fifth note above the key-note.

In the plagal modes, the dominant is the third note below the dominant of the authentic mode, from which the plagal mode is derived.

Both in the authentic and plagal modes when the note "B" is the dominant, the next note to it, that is "C," is taken instead, as in the third and the eighth modes.

The "second" mode is derived from the "first," the "fourth" from the "third," the "sixth" from the "fifth," and the "eighth" from the "seventh."

The Gregorian or Plain Chant as now used, has undergone but little change from its primitive form.

The Greeks called the notes by names very difficult to retain, and expressed them by the most complicated signs.

Pope St. Gregory the Great applied to the notes the names and shapes of the _{Origin of the names of the notes a, b, c, etc.} letters of the alphabet: Capitals expressed the lower octave, small letters the upper, and a double letter the highest sound, thus: A B C D E F G, a ♭b b c d e f g, aa. This is the origin of the names of the notes a b c, etc.

Toward the end of the ninth century, a monk, Hucbald de St. Amand, of _{9th Century.} Flanders, used the perfect consonances of "fourth," "fifth," and "Octave."

Guido d'Arezzo, a Benedictine monk living in the Duchy of Ferrara (Italy,) _{11th Century. Guido d'Arezzo} added four notes to the upper sounds and one to the bass, called "G." To distinguish this new "G" from the others, he represented it by the "gamma," (Γ, g, of the Greeks,) thus: Γ A B C D E F G, a ♭b b c d e f g, aa bb cc dd ee. This new scale took the name of its lowest sound "gamma," and from this the _{Origin of the word Gamut.} word "Gamut" (scale) has its origin.

Setting aside the tetrachordal system, Guido began the new scale with the lowest sound and divided it into seven hexachords; the semitone then came between the third and fourth notes; and Guido, not to change the names of the notes, but only to express the interval between them, applied to the notes the names of " ut," " re," " mi," " fa," " sol," " la," so that to whichever note " ut" was applied, the semitone was always between " mi " and " fa," as will be seen in the " hexachordal system."

(margin note: Origin of the names of the notes "ut," "re," "mi," etc.)

Guido took these names from the first word or first syllable of a Latin hymn in honor of St. John the Baptist, thus: —

Ut queant laxis,
*Re*sonare fibris,
*Mi*ra gestorum,
*Fa*muli tuorum
*Sol*ve polluti,
*La*bii reatum,
Sancte Joannes.

To three sounds only, " F," " C," " G," (the three generator sounds, see " How Music exists in Nature,") did Guido apply the name of " ut."

(margin note: Ut applied to F.)
(margin note: Origin of the word "bemol.")
To " F " in the mol hexachord, so called because in it the " B was mol," that is, soft (flat;) this is the origin of the word " bemol " (flat.)

(margin note: Ut applied to C.)
To " C " in the natural hexachord, so called because in it all the notes were natural.

(margin note: Ut applied to G.)
(margin note: Origin of the word "becarre.")
To " G " in the dur hexachord, so called because in it the " B was quarre " (natural,) that is, dur, hard, compared to the " B mol; " this is the origin of the word " becarre " (natural.)

HEXACHORDAL SYSTEM.

			Mol Hexachord. b mol.	Natural Hexachord. no b.	Dur Hexachord. b quarre.
	ee	mi	. . . .	. . . .	la
	dd	re	. la	. . . .	sol
	cc	ut	. sol	. . . .	fa } semitone.
	bb	si	♭bb fa } semitone.	. .	mi
	aa	la	. mi	la	re
G, is ut. / F, is ut.	g	sol	. re	sol	ut
	f	fa	. ut	fa } semitone. mi	.
	e	mi	. . . .	mi	la
	d	re	. la	re	sol
C, is ut.	c	ut	. sol	ut	fa } semitone. mi
	b	si	♭b fa } semitone.	. .	mi
	a	la	. mi	la	re
G, is ut. / F, is ut.	G	sol	. re	sol	ut
	F	fa	. ut	fa } semitone. mi	.
	E	mi	. . . .	mi	la
	D	re	. . . .	re	sol
C, is ut.	C	ut	. . . .	ut	fa } semitone. mi
	B	si	. . . .	. . . .	mi
	A	la	. . . .	. . . .	re
G, is ut.	Γ	sol	. . . .	. . . .	ut

In the natural hexachord, there was no " B," which note, on account of its allowable alteration to " B flat," was the cause of Guido's applying the names of ut, re, mi, fa, sol, la, to the six notes, c, d, e, f, g, a, which were invariable. Our first scale also begins with " C " both from the natural law, (See " How Music exists in Nature,") and from the natural hexachord. Guido gave no special name to the note " B," because in the mol hexachord it was " fa," in the natural hexachord it did not occur at all, and in the dur hexachord it was " mi."

When the melody extended farther than the hexachord, a change was made *Muances.* from one hexachord to another; these changes were called " muances," from the Latin mutatio; the names of the notes also changed in accordance with the hexachord employed, and as the muances were quite frequent, the hexachordal system was very complicated.

Guido is reputed to be the one who began to express musical sounds by points *Origin of Counterpoint.* (dots) instead of letters. Later, points were placed over or under, or both over and under one given point, all harmonizing with each other, and this is the origin of counterpoint. (See * 14 century; also " Counterpoint," page 14.)

One of the three generator sounds, " F," " C," or " G," (the three sounds to *Origin of the clefs.* which the " ut " was applied in the hexachordal system,) was placed at the beginning of a staff consisting of " four lines," and the notes took their names from their respective places from the letter " F," " C," or " G," placed at the beginning of the staff.

This is the origin of the clefs " F," " C," and " G," and although their shapes have been greatly altered and disfigured with time, we can still recognize in the shape of our clefs, the original shape of the letters " F," " C," and " G." , for F. , for C. , for G.

Jean de Muris, chanoine of Paris, gave to the notes a particular shape, which *• 14th Century.* expressed their value; with this improvement really began the art of counterpoint. By counterpoint was understood a combination of sounds producing an agreeable harmony; considered as a science, it was that treating of the laws that regulated the composition of music. In a word, it expressed then what we express now by the word " harmony." About that time, music for the human voice was divided into four parts, the lowest of which was called " tenor," the next " counter-tenor," the third " metotus," and the highest " triplum or treble."

Music for the human voice is divided into six parts, called " Bass," " Baritone," *16th Century* " Tenor," " Contralto," " Mezzo Soprano," and " Soprano."

The imperfect consonances of third and sixth, were never used, either at the *16th Century.* beginning or end of a piece.

The name of " si " was given by a Flamand to the note " b," thus abolishing *" B " called " si."* the muances and the hexachordal system.

Germany and England preserved the names of the notes, a, b, c, d, e, f, g.

Italy, France, Spain, etc., adopted those of ut, re, mi, fa, sol, la, si.

The staff of five lines is now the one generally used.

Our present system comes from the hexachordal system, but having the liberty to begin a diatonic scale on any given note, it follows that sharps and flats come as a consequence to render the intervals similar to the primitive model.

16th Century. Orlandus Lassus.   Orlandus Lassus, born in Mons, Hainault, in 1520, died in Munich in 1593.

Jacques Hobrecht, Jean Okeghem, and Jean Tinctoris, belong to the illustrious "Flemish School," from which all others originate.

Palestrina.   Giovanni Pietro Alosioda Palestrina, born in Palestrina near Rome, in 1524, died in Rome in 1594. He was the originator of the "Italian School."

17th Century   Claude Monteverde brought in use the chord of "Dominant Seventh."

That chord opened a new era to music, which, however, progressed very slowly for a considerable time.

Conservatories were established in Italy, whose mission was to regulate the laws of music. This proved to be a most ungrateful task, it being almost impossible to come to a clear system between the old and new theories.

"Ut" called "Do."   An Italian named "Doni," applied the first syllable of his name "Do" to the note "ut," as a softer syllable to sing.

G. F. Händel.   George Friedrick Händel, born in Halle, (Prussian Saxony,) February 23, 1685, died in London, April 13, 1759.

J. S. Bach.   Johann Sebastian Bach, born at Eisenach, (Germany,) March 21, 1685, died at Leipzig, July 28, 1750.

J. P. Rameau.   Jean Philippe Rameau, born at Dijon, (France,) in 1683, died in Paris in 1764 ; published in 1722 his treatise of harmony, the first book of the kind ; later, Catel published one somewhat better than Rameau's ; his pupil, M. Dourlen, published a third, improving on the one of his master, but still far from perfection.

18th Century. Gluck.   Christopher Welcbald Gluck, born at Weidlnwang, in the Upper Palatinate, close to the Bohemian boundary, July 2, 1714, died in Weimar, November 15, 1787.

Haydn.   Joseph Haydn, born in Rohran, (Lower Austria,) March 31, 1732, died in Vienna, May 31, 1809.

Mozart.   Johannes Chrysostomus Wolfgang Amadeus Mozart, born in Saltzburg, January 27, 1756, died December 5, 1791.

Cherubini.   Maria Luigi Carlo Zenobi Salvador Cherubini, born in Florence, September 8, 1760, died in Paris, March 15, 1842.

Beethoven.   Ludwig van Beethoven, born in Bonn, on the Rhine, December 16, 1770, died in Vienna, March 26, 1827.

Hummel.   Johann Nepomeck Hummel, born in Presburg, November 14, 1778, died in Weimar, October 17, 1837.

Neukomm.   Chevalier Sigismond Neukomm, born in Saltzburg, July 10, 1778, died in Bonn, April, 1857.

Weber.   Karl Maria Friedrick Ernst, baron von Weber, born at Eutin, (Holstein,) December 18, 1786, died in London, January 5, 1826.

Czerny.   Karl Czerny, born in Vienna, February 21, 1791, died in Vienna, July 15, 1857.

Schubert.   Franz Schubert, born in Vienna, January 31, 1797, died in Vienna, November 19, 1828.

Felix Mendelssohn Bartholdy, born in Hamburg, February 3, 1809, died in 19th Century. Mendelssohn. Leipzig, November 4, 1847.

Frederic Chopin, born at Zelazova-Wola, near Warsaw, in 1810, died in Paris, Chopin. October 14, 1849.

Robert Schumann, born in Zwickau, (Saxony,) January 8, 1810, died July Schumann. 29, 1856.

HOW MUSIC EXISTS IN NATURE.

—◆—

Music exists in nature and originates in a wonderful principle of acoustics, which is, that one sound produces several others, called its harmonic sounds, and accordingly takes the name of generator sound.

To hear this effect of acoustics, the generator sound must be generous in volume. Suppose, for instance, the French horn sounds the note "F," as this sound diminishes in tone, the sounds of "C" and of "A" will be heard. Several other sounds can also be distinguished; we only mention, however, the two most important. The "C" perfect fifth of "F" will be heard as the twelfth sound above the given "F," and the "A" major third of "F," (the major mode is natural, therefore the most perfect,) as the seventeenth sound above the same given "F." Melody comes from that acoustic effect which is also the principle of Harmony.

It is the principle of Harmony because a sound produces its own major third and perfect fifth, and these three sounds are the three notes which compose a perfect chord, thus: the sound "F" gives us the sound "C," its perfect fifth, and the sound "A" its major third, and "F," "A," "C," are the three notes constituting the perfect chord of "F major."

Melody comes from that acoustic effect, because that same effect of acoustics produces the seven sounds which compose a diatonic scale, thus: the sound "F" gives us those of "C" and "A," the sound "C" produced by the sound "F," gives us in like manner those of "G" and "E," and the sound "G" produced by the sound "C," gives us always by the same law those of "D" and "B;" and now we have seven different sounds, thus:

"F" gives us "C" and "A."
"C" gives us "G" and "E."
"G" gives us "D" and "B."

These sounds, placed one after another in the following order, C D E F G A B, form the scale of "C major." Thus the scale of "C" is the production of the three generator sounds, "F," "C," "G."

Every scale has, like the scale of "C," three generator sounds proceeding from the same cause and bearing the same relations to each other.

The three generator sounds in the degrees of the scale, are the sub-dominant,

2

the key-note, and the dominant, which receive the name of "Tonal notes," because they have in themselves, by their harmonic sounds, all the notes which constitute the scale, and, therefore, contain the principle of "tonality." The relations which exist between several different sounds, produce the impression of a particular key, which impression is called "tonality." (See "Sixth Chapter.") Among the three generator sounds, the second one becomes the most important, being the key-note; the first one is a perfect fifth below the second or key-note, is the fourth degree in the scale, and is called " sub-dominant ; " the third one is a perfect fifth above the second or key-note, is the fifth degree in the scale, and is called "dominant." It will be found in the relation of the keys, (See "Twelfth Chapter,") that the second generator sound being the key-note, the first and third generator sounds always are the key-notes of the two major relatives or kindred keys of this second generator sound.

In speaking of this effect of acoustics, we mention it as a fact; our musical system is not wholly established upon it, but it certainly is one of its principles.

MUSICAL SOUNDS AND THEIR PITCH.

Musical sounds* are produced by the vibrations of an elastic and sonorous body. The air being the most elastic of all bodies, receives and instantly communicates them to the ear.

Pitch.   The degree of acuteness or of gravity of a sound is called "Pitch." The pitch is conventional, but when decided upon, the other notes must be in perfect accord with it. The more numerous the vibrations, the more acute is the pitch of the sound; the less numerous the vibrations, the graver is the pitch of the sound.

Large pipes, long and large strings, give the lowest sound; small pipes, short and fine strings, the highest.

A string of a certain length will give a certain sound, the half of that string gives the same sound, but an octave higher, and has twice as many vibrations.

The five sixths of that same string, give the minor third.

The four fifths, the major third.

The three fourths, the perfect fourth.

The two thirds, the perfect fifth, etc.

The lowest musical sound has 32 vibrations in a second, and is the following one, but two octaves lower than here written, thus :

C two octaves lower.

* See " Sound," in *Musical Dictionary.*

The highest musical sound has 16,384 vibrations in a second, and is the following one but two octaves higher than here written, thus:

C two octaves higher.

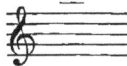

Any sound above or below these two, is no longer a musical sound, but merely a noise.

Thus, all musical sounds are comprised within these two " C "s; they form nine octaves, the highest and lowest of which are rarely if ever used.

The "pitch" was originally a whole tone lower than what is called the "concert pitch," that is to say, the sound which is "A" in the concert pitch, was "B," while "A" of the original pitch became "G" of the concert pitch.

Many voices having been ruined on account of the acuteness of the concert pitch, it was thought advisable to lower it; accordingly, in 1863, it was lowered one semitone; in 1864 all the musicians of the grand opera in Paris were furnished with new instruments, or had their instruments altered to the new pitch, at the expense of the government.

NOISE WHEN PLAYING.

A very disagreeable noise is sometimes heard when playing, which is often thought to come from within the piano, but is really occasioned by the vibrations of the sounds jarring against some object in the room, such as a globe that is loose, or anything of the kind; the very cover of the piano will sometimes jar. By placing something between the piano and the cover, tightening the globe, etc., the noise will cease.

Nothing ought to be left on a piano when playing; music books, pencils, every thing, should be removed. (See "Piano," in *Musical Dictionary*.)

ORCHESTRA.

An orchestra is the reunion of the following instruments : —   Orchestra.

Instruments composing a complete Orchestra.

> Violins, first and second,
> Violas, also called Altos,
> Violoncellos,
> Double basses,
> Flutes,
> Oboes,
> Clarionets,
> Bassoons,
> Horns,
> Trumpets,
> Trombones,
> Timpanis.

An Orchestra is never composed of other than the above-named instruments, which can be multiplied to almost any extent, each one in the right proportion. Triangles, Drums, etc., are occasionally added.

STRING INSTRUMENTS.

Violin. The violin is the leading one among the string instruments, is the highest, and has four strings. Played with a bow.

Viola. The viola is like the violin, but somewhat larger, not so finely shaped, ranges a fifth lower, and plays the tenor part. Also called Alto, or Alto Viol.

Violoncello. A bass-viol, smaller than the double-bass, much larger than the viola, has four strings, the lowest of which is tuned to double " C," that is exactly one octave lower than the viola.

Double-bass. The largest of bass-viols, its tone is very deep, being in pitch an octave lower than the violoncello, and has but three strings. Also called, Contra-basso, Violone, Violono. There are double-bass with four strings, in which case the lowest sound is : one octave lower than here written.

WIND INSTRUMENTS.

Flute. A wind instrument, with holes and keys on the side, made of wood or ivory.

Oboe. A reed wind instrument made of wood, very much like the clarionet, but longer, slender, and thinner in tone.

("Reed," is a little movable tube, or flat vibrating tongue of wood or metal, attached to the mouth of an oboe, clarionet, or bassoon, through which those instruments are blown.)

Clarionet. A reed wind instrument made of wood, very similar to the oboe.

Bassoon. A reed wind instrument made of wood, the bass to the oboe and clarionet.

Horn. A wind instrument generally made of brass.

Trumpet. A wind instrument of the greatest antiquity, made of brass or metal.

Trombone A long, very powerful and sonorous wind instrument made of brass, of the trumpet order, but much larger and with a sliding tube.

Timpani. Kettle-drum, made of two kettles or basins of brass, rounded at the bottom and covered at the top with parchment or goatskin.

MEDIUM COMPASS OF THE INSTRUMENTS COMPOSING THE QUARTETTE STRING.

The double-bass always gives the sounds one octave lower from where written.

We do not give the compass of the other instruments, as it would compel us to enter too much into details.

MEDIUM COMPASS OF THE VOICES.

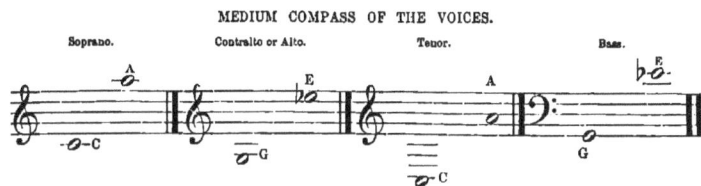

WHAT MUSIC IS COMPOSED OF.

Music is composed of three elements: Rhythm, Melody, and Harmony.

Rhythm, in a general sense, means the measure or the division of time.

In music, it has three different applications: First, Rhythm expresses the Rhythm. relative duration or value of the notes, their particular accent, and the different movement or tempo of a piece. Second, an even division of time is also called Rhythm. Third, Music is written in phrases, sentences, and periods, and any of these may be called a Rhythm.

Hereafter we shall employ the word Rhythm to express the relative duration or value of the notes, their particular accent, and the different movement or tempo of a piece.

The word Measure will be used when referring to an even division of time, that is to say, to the time to be counted in a bar.

A phrase, sentence, or period, will be called a Phrase, a Sentence, or a Period.

Melody is a succession of single sounds: thus, several or even only two different Melody. sounds heard successively form a melody.

Harmony is a combination of several different sounds heard at once. (The Harmony science that treats of the laws which regulate the composition of music, is also called Harmony.)

Rhythm employed as meaning an even division of time, that is, *the measure*, can exist without melody or harmony. One can beat time without either singing or playing; drums beat time. The measure is the most indispensable of the three elements of music, which without it would be nothing but confusion.

Melody can exist without harmony, but cannot dispense with the measure.

Harmony does not really exist, unless combined with melody and measure, for if only two different chords are played at once there is melody; and without measure music cannot exist, therefore there is no harmony.

HARMONY.

Harmony.　Harmony, considered as a science, treats of the laws that regulate the composition of music. Thorough-bass or Figured-bass, Imitation, Canon, Counterpoint, and Fugue, are branches of Harmony.

Thorough-bass or Figured-bass.　A bass being given, the other notes of the chords are indicated by figures, written over the notes of the bass.

Imitation.　A phrase being given by one part, another part repeats that same phrase or a member of it. Imitations generally are composed of short phrases or only members of phrases.

Canon.　A canon is written in two or more parts or voices, thus: a phrase being taken as a subject by one part, is rigorously imitated by another part, thus forming a second phrase, called the imitation of the first; such an uninterrupted imitation is a canon.

Counterpoint.　Counterpoint means " point against point, or note against note," (See " Origin of counterpoint," page 7,) and is written in two or more parts or voices.

Counterpoint is an harmony, the different parts or voices of which can exchange places and form a good bass to the other parts.

There are five kinds of counterpoint, namely : —

　　　　Note against note,
　　　　Two notes against one,
　　　　Four notes against one,
　　　　With syncope and
　　　　Counterpoint fleuri.

Fugue.　A fugue is written in two or more parts or voices, thus :

Subject-phrase.　A " phrase " being taken as a " subject " by one part, another part immediately follows the subject-phrase, with an answer identical to the subject, but in a different key. There may be also, contre-subject, stretto, and pedal.

Contre-subject.　" Contre-subject," is a phrase following the subject-phrase or the answer.

Stretto.　" Stretto " means closer. Stretto is that part of the fugue where the subject and the answer follow each other in close and closer succession, so much so, that finally, one often begins almost as soon as the other ; the stretto is always placed toward the end of the fugue.

Pedal.　There is " ▇▇▇ hen a note (the key-note or the dominant, but generally the dominant) be▇▇▇ ained, the subject, the answer in stretto, contre-subject, etc., are heard in the other parts. The severity of the laws of harmony is greatly diminished when there is " pedal;" unprepared dissonances are heard; new modulations, regardless of the pedal note, may be introduced, provided the first and last bar harmonize with the pedal note.

The fugue is the one composition where all the resources of the art can be combined, according to the musical intelligence, knowledge, will, and ingenuity of the composer.

CLASSICAL AND MODERN MUSIC.

Classical music.　Classical music is that in which the laws of harmony are observed in their full severity and perfection. The combinations are rich and new, every part important; harmonic marches, suspensions,[1] and imitations are frequent; canon, counterpoint, and fugue, belong to it. Two or more parts in unison, enharmonic modulations, broken chords, notes of embellishment, etc., are avoided.

Church music, fugues, and canons, music d'école et d'étude, are classical.

Modern or brilliant music (we only refer to good, though modern music,) is *Modern music.* that in which the laws of harmony are also observed, but not so strictly as in the classical music. There is more liberty as regards modulations, one part alone may be important and the others but secondary; two or more parts in unison, enharmonic marches, etc., are allowed; the resolution of dissonant chords is often irregular; broken chords, successions of thirds, sixths, and octaves, notes of embellishment, etc., are very frequent.

Concertos, solos, airs, romances, rondos, etc., belong principally to modern music.

Some of the works of the great masters combine both the classical and the modern school.

THE DIFFERENCE BETWEEN A SYMPHONY AND A CONCERTO.

A symphony is an orchestral composition in which all the instruments combine *Symphony.* to produce a perfect whole. A symphony has several movements, such as an allegro, an adagio, a scherzo, and a finale, or any other such movements.

A concerto is a musical composition written for any one instrument with *Concerto.* orchestral accompaniment. A concerto has also several movements.

WHAT IS A PARTITION OR SCORE.

A partition or score is the piece of music where all the parts of a musical *Partition or Score.* work are so arranged under each other that at a glance one may follow the whole. On each page there are as many staves as instruments and voices.

The partition of an opera, or of any other such musical work, has often the orchestral part arranged for the piano for greater use and convenience.

METRONOME OF MAELZEL.

The metronome was invented by Winckel of Amsterdam, and was perfected in *Metronome.* 1815 by Maelzel, who gave it his name. The metronome is a ▉▉▉ramidal box about a foot in height, within which is a branch somewhat s▉▉ an inverted pendulum, on which a weight slides up and down at will.

A scale of figures is written on the inside of the box. The unity taken is the minute: if the weight is placed at the number "60," the pendulum will move sixty times in a minute. If placed at the number "200," the pendulum will move two hundred times in a minute, etc.

To indicate the movement of a piece, a note and a number are written at *Its utility.* the beginning, thus: ♩=100. This indicates to slide the weight at the number "100." The pendulum will move a hundred times in a minute, each time being the value of a quarter note.

[1] See "Suspensions," *Musical Dictionary.*

WHO SHOULD TAKE MUSIC LESSONS.

MUSIC elevates the soul, soothes the heart, and is a chaste, useful, and agreeable enjoyment. In Germany, every one learns music ; for generations, the Germans have been a musical nation. Constant cultivation of the musical faculties brings them to the highest degree of refinement.

All those who have great musical talent should of course take music lessons.

Those who have less musical talent should also take music lessons and improve what they have.

Those who have no particular musical talent, provided they have some ear, should also take music lessons, for it is very good and agreeable to be able to play the accompaniment of a song, some dancing music ; and also some pieces to make home pleasant.

Both boys and girls should take music lessons. Girls are expected to devote more time to music than boys, the education of the latter requiring too much of their time to afford a great deal of it to music ; but why deprive boys of a pastime which will prove valuable and refining in after life. Boys go to dancing school, why not to music school ?

WHO IS AN ACCOMPLISHED MUSIC TEACHER.

The one who has the three following qualities : —

First, true knowledge.

Second, the faculty of imparting it.

Third, the one who makes the faithful efforts necessary for success.

HOW TO LEARN TO READ MUSIC AT SIGHT.

Every one can become a good reader of music ; to accomplish it, the following manner is the one adopted in Europe.

All the time that school is attended, half an hour, an hour, an hour and a half, is all the time required (we of course refer only to those who learn music as an accompaniment,) and during those years ; for music ought to be begun at seven or eight years old, and go hand in hand with the school education, without interruption or change of teacher, as far as circumstances admit ; therefore, during the years that school is attended, the teaching aims only at thorough learning, by practising many studies and few pieces ; but when school is over, then about three hours' daily practice is expected, half an hour is devoted to exercises, half an hour to reading music at sight, an hour and a half or two hours to pieces.

New music, slowly and carefully read every day for half an hour, will make a good reader in six months, and a very good one within a year.

A very good and most important rule. Before beginning to play, to answer to one's self the three following questions :

First, in what key is the music written? Second, what is the measure? Third, what is the movement or tempo?

To procure new music every day, a subscription is taken at a music store.

SUBSCRIPTIONS AT MUSIC STORES.

To take a subscription at a music store is to pay five, ten, or more dollars a year, which gives the right to take five or ten dollars' worth of music at a time, and to exchange it every day if desired.

The music taken from the store may be new or old, indifferently, but is expected to be returned in as good order as when taken; if spoiled it is to be paid for. The music must be carried in a flat portfolio, and to mark any fingering is strictly forbidden.

Partitions, and all music for the piano with or without accompaniment, are included in a subscription.

Songs, instruction books, and studies, are not included.

Each music dealer can make his own rules, but these are the ones most generally adopted.

HOW TO HAVE MUSIC BOUND.

A music book should be bound with a "loose back," so as to stand flat open on the desk; it should not be stitched, and it is advisable to have it of a moderate size. — Always have it sewed.

HOW TO PRACTISE TO ACQUIRE THOROUGH LEARNING.

THE lesson given is short and kept in practise as many lessons as it requires, 1st Point. never leaving an exercise, study, or piece, before it is perfectly learned.

Counting to one's self is not sufficient. The counting should be audible and 2d Point. constant, but not so loud as to become fatiguing; however, in passages where it is difficult to keep perfect time, it is preferable, even necessary, to count aloud.

The lesson is read through slowly once or twice, so as to form a general idea 3d Point. of it; then divided into small parts or portions, for instance one phrase or more, (until the eighth chapter is learned, the teacher divides it for the pupil) each part is practised five, ten, twenty, thirty, or more times over, always slowly; the harder the passage the many more times it must be repeated, and a lesser number of bars must be practised together; so much so, that if one bar or two bars were particularly difficult, that one bar or those two bars should be practised by themselves many times over every day: when feeling too tired of the passage, practise another to refresh the mind, but come back to the hard passage again until it is made easy to the fingers. An easy passage needs to be repeated a lesser number of times and more bars may be practised together, but even the

3

easiest piece will be learned more promptly by not practising a whole page at once. Do not slight a piece because it is easy; if it is worth learning, it is worth learning well.

To have the notes, the fingering, and the measure exactly correct, to mark the phrasing only in the most important passages — just as a painter takes a sketch — is all that is to be attended to for the present.

4th Point. The time has come to pay attention to speed. Slow practice brings with itself true and fast improvement; fast practising is worse than none at all; but after the practice has been done slowly and the lesson is thoroughly learned, it is time to pay attention to speed; this must be done by degrees, thus: the lesson is played again slowly two or three times, then a little faster, and a little faster, and so repeating — always increasing the speed until the piece can be played as fast as is required. If any faltering happens when increasing the speed, this shows that the lesson needs a little more slow practice at the passage faltered upon; by the by, when in practising, a passage is missed, never begin the practice of that passage several bars before it, but practise the very passage itself; after it is learned, then join it with the bars before and after it.

5th Point. This is the most interesting part of the study; so far the mechanical part occupied all the attention, now the intellectual part steps in, and having flexible, tractable fingers to deal with, demands good phrasing, that is to say, correct punctuation of the phrases, sentences, and periods, perfect accent, proper accentuation of the rhythm, and the most delicate shades; crescendos, and decrescendos, sudden loud and soft, that is, contrasts; pressing or holding some notes: in a word, that something which is the soul of music, that never exaggerates, but conveys to the hearer the thoughts and ideas contained in the music. After every point of good practising has been complied with, the piece can. be played in company. To have fingers able to do what the mind conceives can really be called "playing." Never attempt to play a piece before it has been duly practised, else there is some danger of failing.

Commit music to memory. To commit music to memory is most desirable, and should always be done, but first learn the piece thoroughly with the notes; after that, and only after that, commit it to memory.

When learning to play without the notes, and a mistake is made, do not try to correct it from memory, but look at the very passage, play it a few times with the music, and then without.

General remarks. 1st. No matter what degree of perfection may have been attained, exercises should never be neglected.

2d. The greater the attention paid to the remarks of the teacher, the greater also the improvement; but to imitate the manners of the teacher, is not desirable; every one ought to have and to keep his own individuality.

3d. In music there are two parts: the mechanical and the intellectual.

4th. Many who have great natural talent never play very well, because by not paying sufficient attention to the mechanism, their fingers are unable to express what they feel and understand.

TOUCH.

—•—

AMONG the many different ways of touching a note, the five principal ones are:

Full Staccato, **' ' '**
Staccato,   · · ·
Legato,
Very Legato,
Extremely Legato.

Full staccato is expressed by a comma placed over or under the note, thus: *Full staccato.* **' ' ' '**

To play " full staccato," is to jump the finger, snapping the note.
Never forget that it is not of a good school to lift the hand too high.
By sliding the finger quickly off the key, a different staccato touch is obtained, which in some cases is desirable.

Staccato is expressed by a dot placed over or under the note, thus: *Staccato.* · · · ·

To play " staccato " is to leave the note before the next one is played, jumping a very little to disconnect the sounds.

Legato is not expressed by any particular sign, but is the touch intended when *Legato.* none is marked. The legato touch is the most important of all, because the one most often used; consequently must be the first to be practised.

To play "legato," is to connect the sounds, thus: place the hands in the proper position (See page 30) and keep the palm of the hand perfectly still, raise the finger as high as possible (while practising to acquire the legato touch, keep the finger up a moment before striking, and be particular to keep it always bent,) then play the note firmly. Do not stutter by half playing a note and playing it again, but strike the note at once. After the note is played, never allow the key to move, by lifting the finger a little, — this also makes the sound stutter, — but hold the note fully down, raise the next finger, (always keeping it bent and do not hurry to play the following note,) then at the same instant that this finger plays the note, leave the one before it.

The motion of a pair of scales gives a very fair illustration of the legato touch. For acquiring strength and flexibility, the legato touch is invaluable.

Very legato is expressed by a slur placed over or under the notes, thus: *Very legato*

To play " very legato " is to hold the note until the following one is played, and then leave it without jumping.

Extremely legato is expressed by a mark, thus : - - - placed over or under

the notes and a slur placed over those marks,
thus :

To play " extremely legato " is to press on the key at the same time that it is played, and hold it down an instant after the next one is played, then to lift the finger just enough to allow the key to rise, and no more.

When a commanding tone is required, strike with the very end of the finger; when extreme sweetness of tone is desired, play with the flat part of the finger; the usual touch being between the two.

Play both hands " square," also lift them " square." To play " square " is to strike the notes at the same instant.

To leave the notes " square," is to leave them at the same instant.

Thirds, sixths, octaves, and chords, must be played " square," and every one of the notes equally loud ; they also must be left " square."

Octaves and chords must be played from the wrist, but when they require to be played with great power, from the elbow; that is, the hand and fore-arm move from the elbow.

If several octaves are to be played successively the hand retains the same position when raised that it had when on the key-board.

Whether a note is to be played loud or soft, if it needs to be struck so that the sound will be short and sharp, touch the note as if to cut it — clear and crisp.

To snap a chord, is to play it with that same touch.

To play loud, the notes or chords are struck either from the knuckles, the wrist, or the elbow.

To play full, the notes or chords are played by pressing on the keys.

When the same notes or chords are required to be repeated without any interruption in the sound, the keys should not be allowed to rise until the very last instant of the beat, and then immediately pressed again without the fingers being lifted from them.

When the notes are far apart, and the hand is too small to reach from one to the other, the note is held to the very last instant of the beat, then the hand glides close to the key-board and as quickly as possible to the next note.

Example

DIFFERENT SIGNS USED WHICH VARY THE TOUCH.

This sign – placed over or under a note indicates to press on the key at the same time that it is played, and when the whole value of the note has expired, to lift the finger just enough to allow the key to rise.

Sometimes the music itself demands that the notes should be played and left in that same manner, although there is no sign.

Either of these signs ⌐ ⌐ ⌐ or . . . . placed over or under a note or notes,

indicates to press on the key at the same time that it is played, and to leave it
before the full value of the note or notes is over.

This sign ∧ placed over or under a note or chord indicates to play with great ∧ ∧ ∧
power, and to be very exact to hold the note or chord the whole of its value.

This sign ⋀ placed over or under a note or chord indicates to play with great ⋀ ⋀ ⋀
power, and to leave the note or chord before its full value is over.

This sign ➤ placed over or under a note or chord indicates to play that note ➤➤➤
or chord louder than the others.

This *sf* indicates to play with force and emphasis.   *sf*

This *rf* indicates to play with still more force and emphasis.   *rf*

It is impossible to write the many different incidents which vary the touch; but Remark.
to touch the note so as to produce the desired sound is the one important thing.

Note. — A comma, thus: ❟ instead of a dot, thus: ❟ or a melodic ornament

not crossed, thus: ♪ when it should be crossed, thus: 𝄞, or any other such mis-
prints, mar somewhat the beauty of the music, and must be rectified when met
with. Always choose the most correct edition.

FINGERING.

⸻✦⸻

Tʜᴇʀᴇ are two kinds of fingering, the German and the English.   Two kinds of
                                                                                  fingering.
In the German fingering the hand is considered to have five fingers; the thumb German.
is the first and the little finger the fifth, thus: thumb, 1 — 2, 3, 4, little finger 5.

In the English fingering, there are four fingers and a thumb; the thumb is English.
marked thus: + and the little finger by the number four, thus: thumb — +, 1,
2, 3, little finger 4.

It is desirable to be familiar with both fingerings, rather than to confine one's
self to either exclusively.

GENERAL RULES AND REMARKS.

The German fingering is the one used in this book.   Rules.

For the fingering of the scales, see pages 70, 71. Remark that there are never Fingering of
                                                                               the scales.
more than seven notes in a diatonic scale, consequently the fingering must be
four fingers and then three; or, three fingers and then four. The exceptions
to this rule are very few, as can be seen on pages 70, 71.

Fingering of C
major scale in
thirds.

For the chromatic scale, the following fingering is the only good one : —

Fingering of the perfect chord. When one of the three notes composing the perfect chord is doubled, whether the chord is played square or arpeggio, the fingering is this: first, second, and fifth fingers are always used; there remain two fingers for the one note left, and this is the rule to be observed: when between the little finger and the next note to it, there is but one white key, the fourth finger must be used, but when there are two white keys, the third finger is used. This rule applies equally to both hands. Example : —

How to correct the over-accentuation of the thumb. If the thumb is too heavy on the note in such a passage as this : —

practise it in marking the accent thus, until the over-accentuation is corrected.

When one of the four notes composing the * dominant seventh chord is doubled, the five fingers are used. Example : —

Fingering of
the dominant
seventh chord.

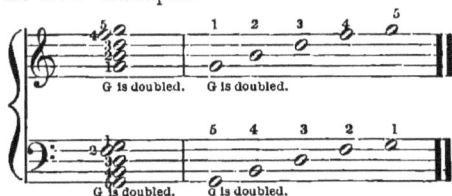

When the hand is too small to play an octave or a chord, let the other hand play some of the notes of that chord or octave ; if it is not possible, the notes to be omitted are the lowest in the right hand and the highest in the left, because the middle notes render the harmony fuller, but are not so essential. Sometimes it is preferable to † run the octave or the chord, rather than to omit some of the notes.

Remarks.
1.

If a note is to be particularly accented, endeavor to have it played by one of the strongest fingers.

2.

To change the fingers is most important, particularly so when some notes are to be held and the hand is small. (See "Changing fingers," page 24.)

3.

The best fingering is that which allows the best playing with the least motion of the hands.

4.

The same passage can be played with different though equally good fingering, according to the size of the hand, its strength or weakness.

5.

When the hand is too small to play the whole of a dominant seventh chord, or of any other such aggregation of notes, the thumb plays two of the notes.

6.

Examples :

When the hand is too weak to play a note with the degree of strength required, it is in particular cases allowable to play that one note with two fingers, one over the other. Example : —

7.

TAKEN FROM BEETHOVEN'S EIGHTH SONATA, op. 13.

crese.

The greatest care must be taken to finger well, as in many cases a passage is missed merely through a fault of fingering.

8.

* See " One Word More," page 73.

† See this sign {, page 24.

VARIOUS SIGNS AND ABBREVIATIONS USED IN MUSIC.

———•———

SIGNS.

THIS sign ⦃ placed before a chord or an octave, indicates that it is to be played arpeggio ; that is, to run the notes in quick succession from the lowest to the highest. (See "Arpeggios or broken chords," page 52.)

If the other hand plays, both hands should fall together on the last note of the arpeggio chord or octave.

This sign ·𝄋· indicates to repeat from where the same sign is written before.

This   indicates that after playing through the bar over which is placed " 1st," what has been played must be repeated from the beginning or from a previous double bar, if there is one. The bar over which is placed " 1st " is not played the second time.

8ᵛᵃ   This " 8ᵛᵃ " placed *over* a passage, thus :

or a note thus :   indicates that such a note or passage is to be played an octave higher than where it is written, whether in the F or G clef.

If placed *under* a note or passage, as sometimes met with in the bass, it indicates that the note or passage is to be played an octave lower than where it is written.

8ᵃ, or 8ᵛᵃ = Ottava, octava, to the octave.

8ᵛᵃ alta. = Ottava alta, an octave higher.

8ᵛᵃ bassa, = Ottava bassa, an octave lower.

Con 8ᵛᵃ, = Con ottava, with octaves.

Loco.   The word " loco " is placed after the " 8ᵛᵃ," thus :   or thus :

to indicate that the notes are to be played where they are written.

Changing fingers. (25) (34) (41) or 𝟤𝟧 𝟥𝟦 𝟦𝟣   Two figures, thus : 𝟤𝟥, 𝟥𝟣, 𝟦𝟣, placed over or under a note, indicate a change of the fingers. In the first example the note is played with the second finger, and the fifth finger takes its place without sounding the note, etc. (See " Remark 3d," page 23.)

⟨ ⟩   See " Crescendo " and " Decrescendo," page 61.

This indicates to remain two bars without playing.

This indicates to remain three bars without playing.

This indicates to remain four bars without playing.

This indicates to remain five bars without playing.

This indicates to remain six bars without playing.

This indicates to remain eight bars without playing.

This indicates to remain the written number of bars without playing.

Ped, indicates to press down the pedal.

Either of these signs indicates to leave the pedal.

This sign ◊ indicates to leave the pedal and instantly to press it down again.

p. ped, or s. ped, or una corda, indicates to press down the damper pedal, (soft pedal.)

tre corde, indicates to leave the damper pedal, (soft pedal.) See " Pedal," also "una corda," in *Musical Dictionary*.

ABBREVIATIONS.

A half note written thus : or is the abbreviation of

sixteenth notes, thus: or and

indicates that sixteenth notes must be played as many times as will equal the value of a half note.

Two bars, thus : or thus : written as in the following examples :

or are the

abbreviation of the four sixteenth notes, and indicate that these four sixteenths are to be played three times more.

. A bar, thus : indicates to repeat the preceding bar ;

thus : the preceding beat, as :

4

thus :

the preceding beats, as :

4.
This :

is the abbreviation of :

5.
This :

is the abbreviation of :

6.
This :

is the abbreviation of :

7.
This :

is the abbreviation of :

8.
This :

is the abbreviation of :

9.
This :

is the abbreviation of :

simili.

10.
This :

is the abbreviation of :

simili.

11.
This :

is the abbreviation of :

For the rule see page 43.   (Same marginal note.)

Meaning of
any figure
written within
a slur

12

* This example is taken from Beethoven's fifth sonata, op. 10, No 1.

FIRST CHAPTER.

—•—

MUSICAL sounds are expressed to the eye by characters, called "Notes." _{Notes.}
In music there are seven notes.

They are called, a, b, c, d, e, f, g. The sound of each note is higher than that of the preceding one.

These seven notes are repeated again and again; their sound is always the same, but their pitch higher. (See Musical Sounds and their Pitch.)

This succession of seven notes is called "Gamut," or "Diatonic Scale." Diatonic scale or Gamut.

Each note of the diatonic scale is a "degree" of the scale, thus: the first note Degrees of the scale. is the first degree, the second note the second degree, etc.

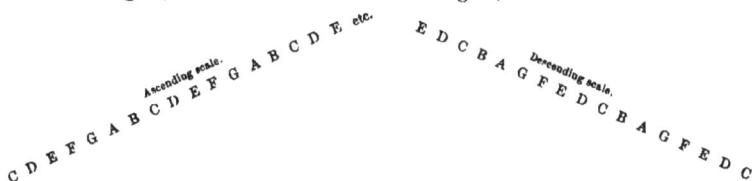

The notes are placed on and between five lines, thus:

The five lines are called "Staff." Example: Staff.

The lower line of the staff is the first line, the upper one is the fifth.

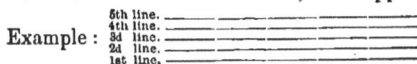

Example : 5th line.
4th line.
3d line.
2d line.
1st line.

The distances between the lines are called "Spaces." Spaces.

Example : 4th space.
3d space.
2d space.
1st space.

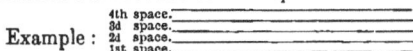

The short lines placed above or below the staff are called "Leger lines." Leger lines.

Example :

Octave of a note.
Key-board.
The eighth note from any given note, is called the "Octave" of that note.

The row of white and black keys upon which one plays, is called "Key-board." A piano has as many octaves as the number of times the seven notes are repeated on the key-board.

* See "Octave," in *Musical Dictionary.*

Clefs.

To ascertain the name of the notes on the staff and their places on the key-board, a character called "Clef" is placed at the beginning of the staff.

In music there are three clefs. They are called: "F" "C" "G."

"F" clef.

The clef of "F" is shaped thus: $\textbf{\large 9:}$ and placed on the fourth line of the staff, thus: The note placed on the fourth line of the staff takes the name of the clef, and is the "F" of the clef; the other notes take their names from their respective places from the clef, in the order of the a, b, c, one note on each line and one note in each space. Example:—

F   f   g   a   b   c   d   e   F   g   a   b   a   g   F   e   d   c   b   a   g   f   F.

Write the clef of "F," be particular to mark very distinctly the note on the fourth line by which it begins, then ascertain its place on the key-board, and learn the name of the notes on the key-board.

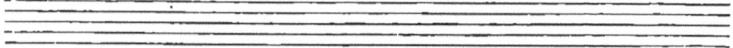

Rule to ascertain the places of the notes on the key-board in either clef.

To ascertain the places of the notes on the key-board, count how many notes above or below the clef they are written, then play them just as many notes above or below the note corresponding to the clef. Example:—

"F"   1   A. 2 notes above F Clef.

1   2   3   4   A. 5 notes below F Clef.

NAMES OF THE NOTES IN THE CLEF OF "F":

LINES.   SPACES.   LEGER LINES.   LEGER LINES.

"F"   g   b   d   "F"   a   "F"   a   c   e   g   "F"   "F"   f   e   d

b   c   d   e

Say aloud the names of the notes of the following line, and find their places on the key-board. Think of the rule mentioned above.

The signs to express the clef of "C" are many, and are used indifferently. "C" clef can be placed on any line but the fifth, and is no longer used for piano music except for transposition. No matter on what line of the staff it is placed, its place on the key-board is always the "C" between the "F" and the "G" clefs. "C" clef is now used for several instruments, mostly those of the middle register.

The clef of " G " is shaped thus : 𝄞 and placed on the second line of the staff, "G" clef.

thus : 𝄞 The note placed on the second line of the staff takes the name of the clef, and is the " G " of the clef; the other notes take their names from their respective places from the clef, in the order of the a, b, c, one note on each line and one note in each space. Example : —

G g f e d c b a G f e d e f G a b c d e f g G.

Write the clef of " G," be particular to begin it on the second line, which is the line of the clef, then ascertain its place on the key-board.

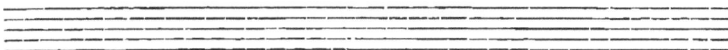

NAMES OF THE NOTES IN THE CLEF OF " G ":

LINES.   SPACES.   LEGER LINES.   LEGER LINES.

"G" e "G" b d f   "G" f a c e   "G" d c b a
                                  "G" g a b c

Say aloud the names of the notes of the following line and find their places on the key-board. Remember the rule mentioned page 28.

The distance from one vertical line to the next is called a " Bar." Bar.

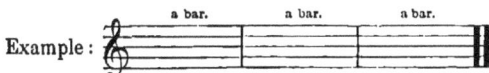

a bar.   a bar.   a bar.

Example :

A double bar indicates the end of an exercise of a piece or of a part of a piece. Example :

Two dots placed by a double bar indicate to repeat the preceding passage or exercise. Example :

Music is generally written in two parts, the " Bass " and the " Treble." The Music written in two parts. bass is written in the clef of " F," and played with the left hand, the treble is written in the clef of " G," and played with the right hand.

POSITION AT THE PIANO.

The seat must be high enough to allow the elbows to be on a level with the key-board, and the distance from the piano must be such that the hands being on the key-board the elbows fall easily on each side of the figure, which should be perfectly erect. Occupy but half the stool, that some weight may rest on the floor.

POSITION OF THE HANDS.

The thumb and the little finger must be placed about in the middle of the white key, the wrist and the knuckles on a level, and the three remaining fingers bent so as to make a curve from the knuckles to the end of the fingers. The knuckles of the fingers naturally will be a little lower than the knuckles of the hand. The fingers must be kept apart so as to be independent of each other.

EXERCISES.

Play the exercises "legato," thus: keep the palm of the hand perfectly still, raise the finger as high as possible (keep the finger up a moment before striking, and be particular to keep it always bent,) then play the note firmly. Do not stutter by half playing a note and playing it again, but strike the note at once. After the note is played never allow the key to move, by lifting the finger a little, as this also makes the sound stutter; but hold the note fully down, raise the next finger, always keeping it bent, and do not hurry to play the following note; then at the same instant that finger plays the note, leave the one before it.

Common time, four beats and four quarter notes in a bar; one quarter note for each beat. (See "1st point," of How to Practise to Acquire Thorough Learning, page 17.)

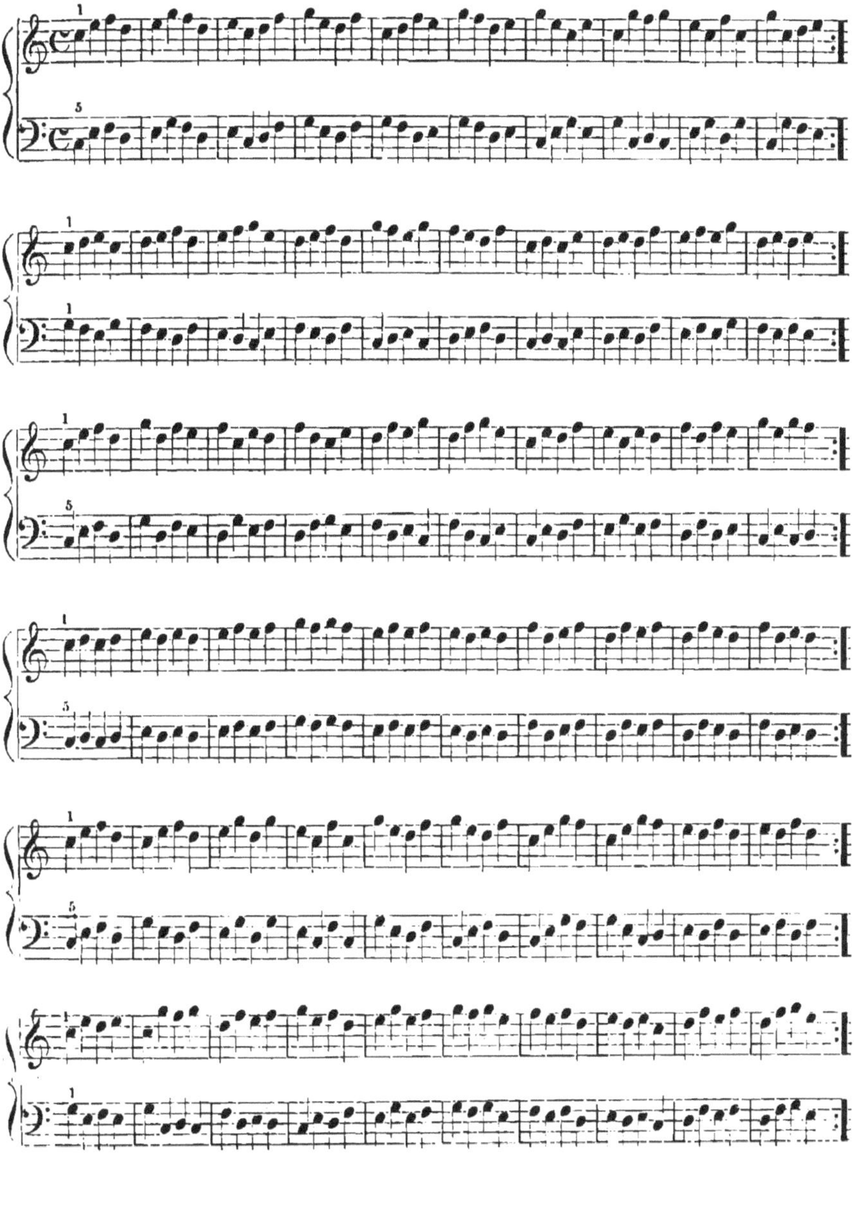

* 8ᵛᵃ.. loco.

* See " 8ᵛᵃ " also " Loco " page 24.

SECOND CHAPTER.

————

In the value of the notes, the unit taken is the " Whole note ; " divided in two, it makes two halves ; in four, it makes four quarters ; in eight, it makes eight eighth notes, etc.

The value of the notes is expressed by their shapes, thus : —

A circle	$\circ$	Whole note,	Shape of the notes.
A circle and stem		Half note,	
A black dot, and stem		Quarter note,	
A black dot, stem, and 1 dash		Eighth note,	
A black dot, stem, and 2 dashes		Sixteenth note,	
A black dot, stem, and 3 dashes		Thirty-second note,	
A black dot, stem, and 4 dashes		Sixty-fourth note.	

Rests take the place of notes, and while their value is counted, the hands must he taken from the key-board.

The value of the rests is expressed by their shapes, thus : —

A bar under the fourth line		Whole note rest,	Shape of the rests.
A bar above the third line		Half note rest,	
An inverted 7 or inverted Z		Quarter note rest,	
A stem and 1 dash		Eighth note rest,	
A stem and 2 dashes		Sixteenth note rest,	
A stem and 3 dashes		Thirty-second note rest,	
A stem and 4 dashes		Sixty-fourth note rest.	

COMPARISON BETWEEN THE SHAPES OF THE NOTES AND RESTS.

Notes.

Rests.

Remark that the eighth note has one dash, the eighth note rest has also one dash ; the sixteenth note has two dashes, as has also the sixteenth note rest, etc.

Lengthening of a dash. A bar, thus : ━━ is the lengthening of a dash to connect two or more notes.

Example : two eighth notes, may be written thus : ♪ ♪ or thus : ♫

How to observe the value of a note or of a rest. Every note of a piece must be held down the whole of its value and no more, and the exact value of every rest must also be observed.

TABLE OF THE VALUE OF THE NOTES.

As the notes increase in number they diminish in value, thus : the note before, is always the double in value ; the note after, always the half. Example : the double of a half note is a whole note, the note before it ; the half of a half note is a quarter note, the note after it.

Dot. A dot after a note or rest, thus : ⟨music⟩ increases the value of that note or rest one half.

Two dots. A second dot placed after the first one, thus : ⟨music⟩ increases the

Examples : value of the first dot one half.

1st. A dot after a whole note, as in the first example, is equal to a half note, because a half note is the half of a whole note.

A dot after an eighth note rest, as in the second example, is equal to a sixteenth note, because a sixteenth note is the half of an eighth note.

A dot placed after another dot, as in the third example, is equal to a quarter note, because a quarter note is the half of a half note, value of the first dot after the whole note, etc.

A slur over two notes of the same name, such as two "G's," or two "C's," makes the second note tied; that is to say, the second note is held the whole of its value but not played.

EXERCISES.

Wherever any note may be placed in a bar, it should always be played according to its value.

Common time; four beats and four quarter notes in a bar, one quarter note for each beat. (See "1st point," of How to practise, etc., page 17.)

Three beats and three quarter notes in a bar, one quarter note for each beat.

* See " 8va....," also " Loco," page 24.

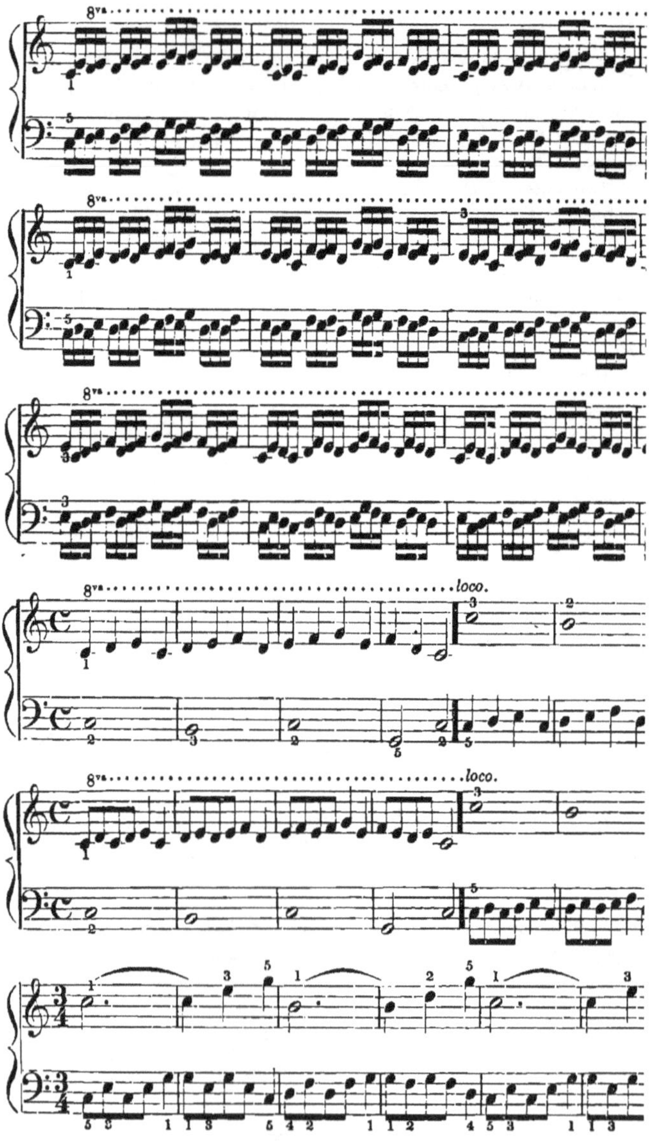
8va
8va
8va
8va
loco.
8va
loco.

THIRD CHAPTER.

AN interval is the distance between two notes, that is, between their different *Interval.* pitch. (See "pitch," page 10.)

A semitone is the smallest interval there is in music. From "B" to "C," or *Semitone* from "E" to "F," there is a semitone. Between any other two white keys, the *Half tone.* distance of sound is greater.

A tone is composed of two semitones. From "C" to "D," or from "G" to *Tone.* "A," there is a tone.

An accident is a sign placed before a note, to alter its pitch. *Accidents.*

In music there are three accidents; they are: the sharp, the flat, and the natural.

The sharp is shaped thus: ♯ and raises the note one semitone; therefore, when *Sharp.* a sharp is placed before a note, that note must always be played on the next ♯ key above.

In music there are seven sharps; they come in the following order: —

"F," "C," "G," "D," "A," "E," "B."

Why they come in the preceding order will be explained in the Tenth Chapter.

The flat is shaped thus: ♭ and lowers the note one semitone; therefore, when *Flat.* a flat is placed before a note, that note must always be played on the next key ♭ below.

In music there are seven flats; they come in the following order: —

"B," "E," "A," "D," "G," "C," "F."

Why they come in the preceding order will be explained in the Tenth Chapter.

The natural is shaped thus: ♮ and brings the note back to its former place, *Natural.* that is, to the place it occupied before it was made either sharp or flat. There ♮ are as many naturals as there are notes, that is, seven.

An accident belongs to the note before which it is placed.

Example :

Remark that the line runs through the accident if the note to which it belongs is on the line; but if the note is in a space the accident also is placed in the space.

DOUBLE SHARPS AND DOUBLE FLATS.

The double sharp is shaped thus: ×, thus: ×, thus: ♯ or thus: ♯♯ and raises *Double sharp.* the note two semitones. ×

The double flat is shaped thus: ♭♭ and lowers the note two semitones. *Double flat.* ♭♭

When a note that is double sharp or double flat, is wanted single sharp or *How expressed when wanted single sharp or single flat.*

single flat, it is expressed thus :

EXERCISES.

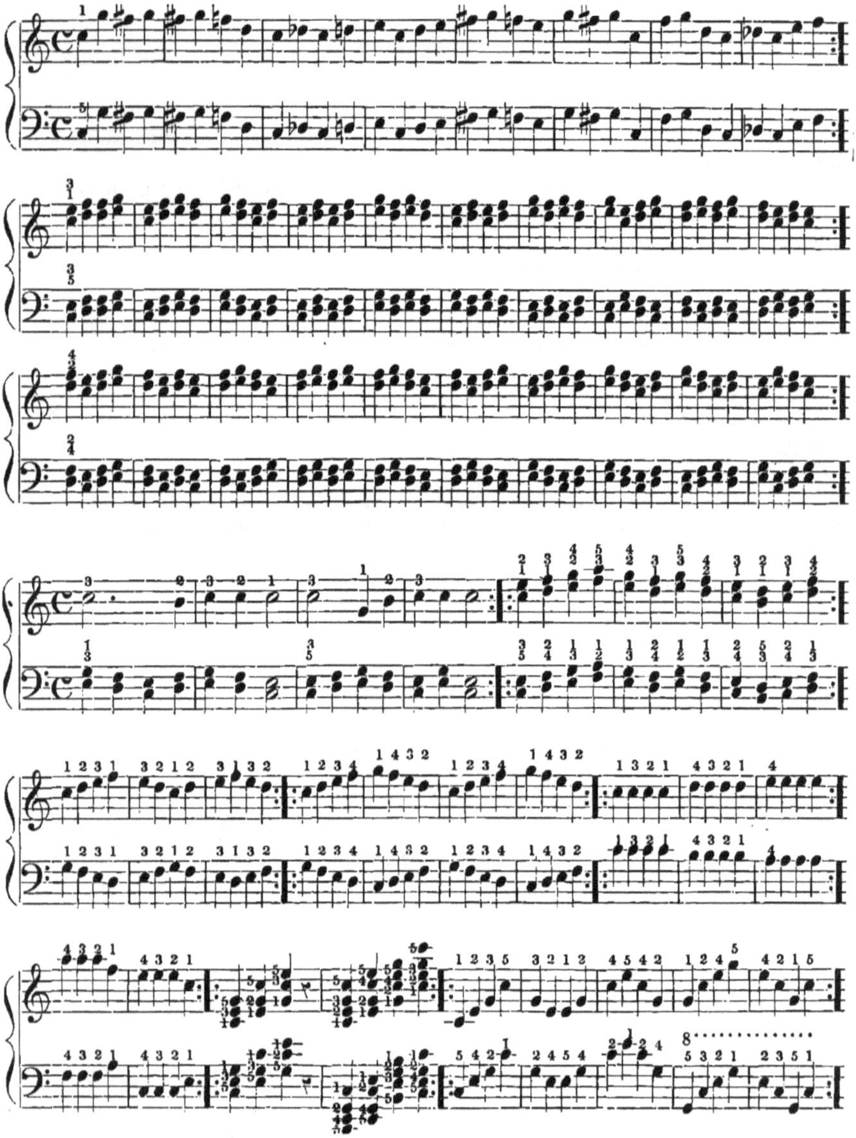

* See 8va · · · · · · · · · ·, also Loco, page 24.

FOURTH CHAPTER.

THREE of the most necessary things to understand in music are : —
First, the clefs.
Second, the signature.
Third, the measure.
The clefs have been explained in the First Chapter, page 28.

Signature. The signature is the name given to the accidents, either ♯ or ♭, placed next to the clefs to indicate the key in which the music is written. (See "Key," page 49.)

The accidents of the signature belong to the notes of the lines or spaces on which they are written, and must be observed throughout the piece, unless altered by an accidental accident. (See "Accidental Accident.")

Alteration of a note. A note is altered when an accident is placed before it.

Any accident, whatever it may be : ♯, ✕, ♭, ♭♭, ♮, placed before a note, alters that note.

The accidents of the signature do not alter the notes to which they belong, for they are themselves real notes of the key in which the music is written.

Accidental accident. Any accident met in a piece and not belonging to the signature, is an accidental accident, and alters the note through one bar.

Sign of precaution. Of late years it has become customary, when the altered note is wanted in its former place, whether in the next bar or even further on, to place an accident before it. Such an accident is called "a sign of precaution."

Measure. The measure is the name given to two figures written one above the other, thus : $\frac{2}{2}$ or $\frac{2}{4}$ or $\frac{3}{8}$ or $\frac{6}{8}$ etc., placed next to the signature, or next to the clef if there is no signature, to indicate the time to be counted in each bar throughout the piece ; but if two different figures are met with, the counting of the measure changes accordingly.

The measure divides music into short portions of equal value, called bars, (See "Bar," page 29,) which are themselves subdivided into shorter portions of equal value, called beats. (See "Example," also "Analysis of the measure," page 41.)

The measure is written with two figures, as explained above ; the upper figure expresses the number of beats and of notes contained in the measure ; the lower figure expresses the value of these notes.

The lower figure signifies the value of the note which it represents, thus : — 2 half notes make a whole note ;
4 quarter notes make a whole note ;
8 eighth notes make a whole note ; etc.

Therefore, the figures 2, 4, 8, etc., when placed underneath, represent the value of "half note," "quarter note," "eighth note," etc.

Example: $\frac{2}{4}$ the upper figure " **2** " indicates that in this measure there are two beats and two notes; the lower figure " **4** " indicates that the value of these notes is to be "quarter note." Therefore, in this measure, there are two beats and two quarter notes, one quarter note for each beat.

The upper figure always answers to the question of number. How many?
The lower figure to the question of value. What kind of note?

In the above example : $\frac{2}{4}$

How many beats?—————————————————————
How many notes?————————————————————Two $\frac{2}{4}$
What kind of note?—————————————————Quarter note.

Therefore, this measure is composed of two beats and two quarter notes, one quarter note for each beat.

The measure $\frac{2}{2}$ or **2** or $\math“C$, two half notes in a bar, is called "Alla breve," Alla breve. because it is a measure of four quarter notes, shortened for the counting. $\frac{2}{2}$ or **2** or $\math“C$

The measure $\frac{4}{4}$ or **4** or **C**, four quarter notes in a bar, is so very often used Common time. that it is called "Common time," and is almost always written thus: **C**, first $\frac{4}{4}$ or **4** or **C** letter of the word "Common" instead, of the two figures $\frac{4}{4}$.

To analyze, is to find the exact value of each beat. For instance, suppose the Analysis of the measure. measure $\frac{2}{4}$: one quarter note or its equivalent must be found for each beat; if the note is more than a quarter note, it must be divided into quarter notes as far as its value permits; if the note is less than a quarter note, others must be added to it until the value of a quarter note is complete.

Example :

First, a quarter note, enough for a beat "one," next an eighth note, (half of a How to analyze. quarter, not enough for a beat,) then a dot, (a dot after a note increases its value one half,) half of an eighth note is a sixteenth, therefore, a dot after an eighth note is equal to a sixteenth; next to the dot is a sixteenth note, (always add together, when it is possible, the notes of the same value,) a sixteenth note added to the dot equal to a sixteenth, makes two sixteenths equal to an eighth note, which added to the eighth note before the dot, makes two eighth notes equal to a quarter note, enough for a beat "two."

Next bar. First, a half note, equal to two quarter notes, too much for a beat, just enough for two, "one" "two."

In the following example the value of some of the notes has to be divided between two beats, and the notes of the same value cannot be added together.

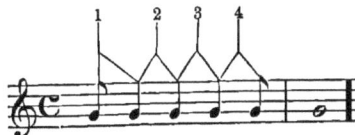

How to analyze the first bar of a piece. When the value of the measure is not complete in the first bar of a piece, the beats or beat, or part of the beat wanting, (whether expressed or not by rests,) are counted before playing the note or notes written.

Examples, where the beats wanting are expressed by rests.

Same examples, where the beats wanting are not expressed by rests.

Music may be written in two, three, four, or more parts. Music is generally written in two parts, as said in the First Chapter, (page 29,) but it may also be written in more, as proved by analyzing. When in a bar there are found notes or rests exceeding the value of the measure, there are as many parts as the number of times the value of the measure can be counted.

*Example in *three* parts.   *Example in *four* parts.

Triplet. A triplet is three notes played in the time of two. The three notes are connected thus : ♪♪♪, a figure "₃" written within a slur is placed either over or under them, thus : ♪♪♪ or thus : ♪♪♪

Two eighth notes are equal to a quarter note.

A triplet of eighth notes is also equal to a quarter note.

Thus : ♪♪ equal to a ♩ as also : ♪♪♪ or ♪♪♪ equal to a ♩

The three notes of the triplet are played a little faster than the two eighth notes, so as to occupy the same time.

Exception. The figure "₃" and even the slur itself are at times omitted, but the notes are always connected thus : ♪♪♪ or thus : ♪♪♪

* These two Examples are taken from Bach's fugues, 2d and 1st.

A figure "₆," written within a slur placed over or under the notes, indicates a Double triplet.
double triplet. The same notes, with the slur, but without the figure "₆," should
be played according to their value ; however, the slur only may be found over a
double triplet, in which case the measure will distinguish between the two. (See
" General Rules for the Grammatical Accent," page 58.)

Any figure, written within a slur placed over or under notes, indicates that Meaning of any figure written within a slur.
those notes are to be divided among the beats over which they are written.

EXAMPLE, TAKEN FROM CHOPIN, OP : 9, NO 1.

Also see another example of same rule, page 26, (same marginal note.)

EXERCISES.

In the following exercises the whole notes are to be pressed down and held but not played.

* See "Remarks," page 47.

In the first two lines the melody is in the bass, and the harmony in the treble; play the treble very soft, that the spirited and cheerful melody may be distinctly heard.

Allegro con spirito. ♩ = 152.   (See "Metronome of Maelzel," page 15.)   R. SCHUMANN. Opus 68.

*See " Changing Fingers," page 24.

In the following line the bass and the treble each have a melody; play the middle part very soft, it being only an accompaniment. (See "Music may be written in two, three, four or more parts," page 42.)

* These two notes being taken by the left hand will allow the melody to be played more Legato.
† If the hand is small, the same will apply to these two F's.

REMARKS. — 1. See "Duvernoy's Studies" in Introduction, page 1.

2. See "A very good and most important rule," page 16.

3. Make it a point to understand the meaning of every term met with in music; for this, look out every word in "Musical Dictionary." (See "Note" in *Musical Dictionary*, page 93.)

FIFTH CHAPTER.

IN music there are but two kinds of measure: the "binary," or direct, and the "ternary," or indirect. _{Two kinds of measure.}

The binary or direct measure has two beats in a bar. Measures of four and eight beats are derived from it. _{Binary or direct.}

In the binary or direct measure and those derived from it, the accent falls evenly on every other beat. (See "Rules for the Grammatical Accent," page 58.)

The ternary or indirect measure has three beats in a bar. Measures of six, nine and twelve beats are derived from it. _{Ternary or indirect.}

In the ternary or indirect measure and those derived from it, the accent falls on the first beat and on every third beat from it. (See "Rules for the Grammatical Accent," page 58.)

The measure is sometimes to be counted differently from what it is written. The rhythm of the piece will tell when to do so. (See "Rhythm," page 56.) For instance, in certain cases, a measure of four beats will be counted _{Change in the counting of the measure.}

eight beats in a bar. Example: when a grave movement is marked C, common time, it is better to change the four quarter notes into eight eighth notes, thus counting eight eighth notes in a bar, instead of four quarter notes. Accent of binary measure.

A measure of four beats will also be counted two beats in a bar, instead of four, according to the movement or tempo of the music. Accent of binary measure.

A measure composed of six eighth notes, as in a "Tarentelle," is to be counted two beats in a bar, three eighth notes for each beat. It does not change the eighth notes into triplets, but leaves them their real value. Accent of binary measure.

To make counting easier to beginners, a $\frac{2}{4}$ measure may be counted $\frac{4}{8}$.

The measure is either simple or compound. _{Simple or compound measure.}

The measure is simple, when composed of the value of the notes themselves, such as half notes, quarter notes, eighth notes, etc. _{Simple.}

The measure is compound, when composed of dotted notes, such as dotted half notes, dotted quarter notes, dotted eighth notes, etc. _{Compound.}

TABLE OF THE SIMPLE AND COMPOUND MEASURES MOST COMMONLY USED.

Difference in the notation of a dotted quarter note changed into eighth notes from a triplet of eighth notes.

A dotted quarter note changed into eighth notes, is written thus: ♪ ♪ ♪ or thus: ♫ ♪ rarely thus: ♫♪ and is equal to three eighth notes; that is, a quarter note and an eighth note.

A triplet is written thus: ♪ 3 ♪ or thus: ♩♩♩ (see "Triplet," page 42,) and is equal to a quarter note.

SIXTH CHAPTER.

IN music there are three orders : namely, the "diatonic," the "chromatic," and Three orders or genera.
the "enharmonic." (See "Genus," "Genera," in *Musical Dictionary*.)

The diatonic order progresses by intervals of tones and semitones. Diatonic order.

Seven notes played in the diatonic order form a diatonic scale. Diatonic scale.

In a diatonic scale there are five tones and two semitones, altogether twelve semitones.

The same seven notes which form a diatonic scale, when played in chords, Key.
runs, etc., as in a piece, are expressed by the word "Key." Naturally, both scale
and key of the same name have the same signature.

The chromatic and the enharmonic orders are also called scale, although the Remark.
word scale, according to rule, belongs only to the diatonic order.

The chromatic order progresses by semitones. Chromatic order.

The enharmonic order is simply the same sound called by two different names, Enharmonic order.
such as C$\sharp$ or D$\flat$, D$\sharp$ or E$\flat$, etc. Two such notes are enharmonic of each other.

In reality there exists a sound for each one of these notes, C$\sharp$ being a little
higher, and D$\flat$ a little lower than the one sound that answers for both in the
enharmonic order ; suppose a tone is divided in nine parts, thus : —

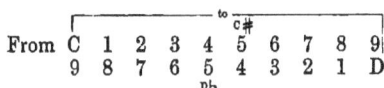

```
                          to  c♯
       From C  1  2  3  4  5  6  7  8  9
              9  8  7  6  5  4  3  2  1  D
                          Db
```

C$\sharp$ is five parts above C, and D$\flat$ five parts below D.

The distance between two such sounds is so minim that to simplify certain
instruments, in particular those having a key-board, the difference is equally
divided in order to make one key answer for the two notes, thus :

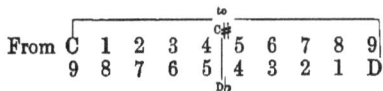

```
                          to
                          c♯
       From C  1  2  3  4 | 5  6  7  8  9
              9  8  7  6  5| 4  3  2  1  D
                          Db
```

On other instruments, the violin for instance, the sound of such two notes have
their true pitch, but when playing with the piano, they also make one sound
answer for the two notes.

There are two kinds of semitones : the diatonic and the chromatic. Two kinds of semitones.

The diatonic semitone is the one between two notes of different names, as Diatonic semitone.
between C and D$\flat$ or F$\sharp$ and G. (Play these notes on the key-board.)

The chromatic semitone is the one between two notes of the same name, as Chromatic semitone.
between C and C$\sharp$ or G$\flat$ and G. (Play these notes on the key-board.)

C major scale,
first diatonic
scale.

The seven fundamental notes or sounds form the first diatonic scale : C major.

Example :

The scale of C major is the model of all the other major scales, that is to say, that a scale to be major, must have its intervals exactly like those of C major scale.

Degrees of the
scale have a
special name.

Each note of a diatonic scale is a degree of that scale, as said in the First Chapter, and each degree has a special name.

The names given to the degrees of the scale express either their function, importance, or merely their places.

NAMES OF THE DEGREES OF THE SCALE.

```
 * 1st degree,  . . . . . . . . Key-note.
   2d degree,  . . . . . . . . Sus-Key-note.
 † 3d degree,  . . . . . . . . Mediant.
 * 4th degree, . . . . . . . . Sub-Dominant.
 * 5th degree, . . . . . . . . Dominant.
   6th degree, . . . . . . . . Sus-Dominant.
 † 7th degree, . . . . . . . . Leading note.
   8th degree, . . . . . . . . Key-note to the octave.
```

EXAMPLE IN THE SCALE OF C MAJOR.

1st half of the scale.
1st degree.   2d degree   3d degree.   4th degree.   2d half of the scale.
5th degree.   6th degree.   7th degree.   8th degree.

Key-note.   Sus-Key-note.   Mediant.   Sub-Dominant.   Dominant.   Sus-Dominant.   Leading-note.   Key-note to the Octave.

These names are applicable to the degrees of every diatonic scale ; hence the first degree of any diatonic scale is called key-note, the second sus-key-note, etc.

The scale may be divided into two halves ; the key-note begins the first half, and the dominant the second half.

Key-note,
1st degree.

* The key-note is the most important degree of the scale : it is the one on which the scale is built.

Dominant,
5th degree.

* The dominant is one of the most important degrees of the scale. (See "Tonal notes," also "Relative or Kindred Keys of Major Scales," page 72.)

Sub-dominant,
4th degree.

* The sub-dominant is also an important degree. (See "Tonal notes," also "Relative or Kindred Keys of Major Scales," page 72.)

Mediant,
3d degree.

† The mediant is the note which determines the mode. (See "How to distinguish the Major mode from the Minor," page 68.)

Leading note,
7th degree.

† The leading note leads to the key-note. Its affinity for the key-note is so strong, that when heard, the key-note at once is desired by the ear.

The other notes take their names from their places.

The key-note, dominant, and sub-dominant, are called " Tonal notes," because Tonal notes. they have in themselves, by their harmonic sounds, (See " How Music exists in Nature,") all the notes which constitute the scale, and therefore give more than any others the impression of the " tonality," that is to say, that more than any other notes they make the ear sensible of the key in which the music is written.

Tonal notes

The relations which exist between several different sounds produce the Tonality. impression of a particular key, which impression is called " Tonality."

It is not necessary to hear the seven notes or sounds of a scale to know to which key they belong. Examples : the seven sounds c, d, e, f, g, a, b, belong to the key of C major ; if only four sounds are heard, for instance

at once the ear searches for the one particular sound to which the others are related, that is the key-note, which in this case is " C."

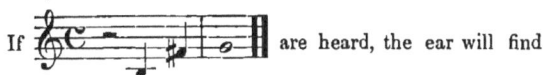

If are heard, the ear will find

that " G " is the one particular sound to which the others are related ; therefore, in the first example a, g, b, c, bring to the ear the tonality of C major ; while in the second example, b, f sharp, g, give the tonality of G major.

When the mediant is not heard, as in the first example, the ear always under- Observation. stands the key to be major. (See " Mediant," also " How Music exists in Nature.")

The need of tonality is so indispensable to the human ear, that a single sound heard is at once received by it as the key-note.

Three, four, or five different notes belonging to the same key, and which can Chord. be placed by intervals of thirds, (See " Intervals," page 53,) when heard at the

same instant, form a " Chord." Example :

It is agreed to call " chord " any aggregation of notes played together, but the rule is that only those notes which belong to the same key and can be placed by intervals of thirds, have the right to be so called.

A chord of three notes can be built on every one of the degrees of the scale.

Thus :

The note on which the chord is built, receives the name of " Fundamental." Fundamental.

Direct state of a chord. A chord is in the direct state when its fundamental is in the bass, thus : — *Perfect chord of C major in the direct state.*

• Positions of a chord. A chord has as many positions as it has notes; for instance, the chord built on the first degree of the scale of C has three positions. (C is the key-note.)

Example :

First position.   Second position.   Third position.

Funda—mental.
Dominant.   Key-note.   Mediant.
Mediant.   Dominant.   Key-note.
Key-note.   Mediant.   Dominant.

Whatever is the place of the fundamental in the different positions of a chord, it always preserves its name and character of fundamental.

In the above example the key-note is the fundamental.

How to recognise a perfect chord. Any three notes which are or can be placed by intervals of thirds, one of which is major, (See "Table of the Intervals," page 53,) and the other minor, (See "Alteration of the Major Intervals," page 54,) are a "perfect chord."

Examples :   1st   2d

In the first example, the first third from C to E is major, the second third from E to G is minor; it is a perfect major chord. (See "Mediant," page 50.)

In the second example, the first third from A to C is minor, the second third from C to E is major; it is a perfect minor chord. (See "Mediant," page 50.)

Arpeggios or broken chords. Arpeggios, or broken chords, are chords whose notes are played successively.

Examples :   1st   2d

Arpeggios, exercises on the Dominant Seventh chord, which chord is explained page 73.

* Changing the position of a chord produces an inversion. (See "Inversion of the Intervals," page 54.)

SEVENTH CHAPTER.

———◆———

THE diatonic scale is divided into " intervals." (See " Interval," page 37.) Intervals.

An interval is reckoned from the key-note to any other note, counting the key-note as " one," or first note. How to reckon an interval.

The " number of notes," that is, the number of degrees, gives the name to the interval, for instance, two degrees of a diatonic scale, as from C to D, make a second, and three degrees, as from C to E, make a third. What gives the name to an interval.

The " number of semitones " determines the quality of the interval. What determines the quality of an interval.

The " quality " of an interval is to be either " perfect," " major," " minor," " augmented," or " diminished." What is the quality of an interval.

The quality of an interval in its first state is either perfect or major. What is the quality of an interval in its first state.

Example : —

TABLE OF THE INTERVALS IN THE SCALE OF C MAJOR.

From.	Number of Notes.	Name of the Intervals.	Number of Semitones.	Quality of the Intervals.
C	1	Unison*	None	perfect.
C to d	2	Second	2	major.
C to e	3	Third	4	major.
C to f	4	Fourth	5	perfect.
C to g	5	Fifth	7	perfect.
C to a	6	Sixth	9	major.
C to b	7	Seventh	11	major.
C to c	8	Octave	12	perfect.

* The unison is not an interval; however, it must be considered as such, else Remark. the rule of " the number of notes, that is, the number of degrees, gives the name to the interval," is destroyed, and besides when inverted (See " Inversion of the Intervals," page 54,) the unison produces an interval of octave.

Intervals are " simple " or " compound," " melodic " or " harmonic."

An interval is simple when contained within the octave. Simple interval.

An interval is compound when extending beyond the octave, being but the Compound interval. repetition of a simple interval to one or more octaves.

Examples :

Simple interval.   Compound interval.

In the above examples the interval of ninth is but the repetition of the second to the octave.

An interval is melodic when its sounds are heard successively, thus : — Melodic interval.

An interval is harmonic when its sounds are heard at once, thus : Harmonic interval.

Alteration of the intervals. The quality of an interval changes according to its number of semitones; an interval thus changed is "altered."

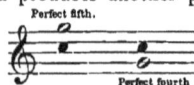

Perfect fifth.

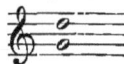

Alterations of the perfect intervals. Every perfect interval can be "augmented" and "diminished."

Augmented fifth.

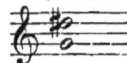

Augmented by adding one chromatic semitone, thus :

Diminished fifth.

Diminished by taking off one chromatic semitone, thus :

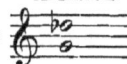

Alterations of the major intervals. Every major interval can be "augmented," "minor," and "diminished."

Major third.

Augmented third.

Augmented by adding one chromatic semitone, thus :

Minor third.

Minor by taking off one chromatic semitone, thus :

Diminished by taking off a second chromatic semitone.

The semitone is always added to or taken off from the upper degree of the interval, except when the major interval is diminished.

To render the "major" interval "minor," one semitone is taken from its upper degree ; a degree can be raised or lowered once only, therefore the second semitone must be taken from the lower degree of the interval. The lower degree of the interval being raised one semitone, the major interval loses a second semitone, and thus becomes diminished.

Diminished third.

Example :

Perfect consonances. Perfect intervals are perfect consonances, because they cannot be altered and remain consonant, but when altered produce a dissonance or discord.

Imperfect consonances. The third and sixth are imperfect consonances, because they can be altered and remain consonant.

Dissonances. The second and seventh are dissonances, because when played they produce a discord.

Inversion of the intervals. When the lower degree of an interval is placed above the upper one, or the upper degree below the lower one, the interval is "inverted." (The same applies to chords.) Examples :

Inversion of the perfect intervals. Every perfect interval when inverted produces another perfect interval. For this reason it is "perfect."

Perfect fifth.

Example :

Perfect fourth

Every major interval when inverted produces
a minor interval. . . . . Example:

Major third.

Minor sixth.

Inversion of the major intervals.

Every minor interval when inverted produces
a major interval. . . . . Example:

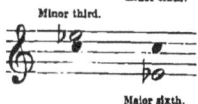

Minor third.

Major sixth.

Inversion of the minor intervals.

The major intervals are so called because they are larger, and the minor ones
because they are smaller.

Every augmented interval when inverted
produces a diminished interval. . . . . Example:

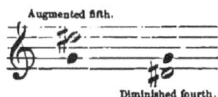

Augmented fifth.

Diminished fourth.

Inversion of the augmented intervals.

Every diminished interval when inverted
produces an augmented interval. . . . . Example:

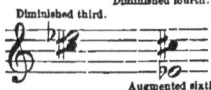

Diminished third.

Augmented sixth.

Inversion of the diminished intervals.

The words "augmented" and "diminished" explain themselves.

A simple interval being inverted always makes the number "nine" when
added to the interval it produces. The reason is this: there are seven notes in
the scale, and when an interval is inverted two of these notes are counted
twice, thus: from C to D is a second, and from D to C is a seventh — seven
and two make "nine;" a second when inverted always produces a seventh, and
a seventh a second. From C to E is a third, and from E to C is a sixth — six
and three make "nine;" a third when inverted always produces a sixth, and
a sixth a third.

The semitones of a simple interval always make the number "twelve" when
added to those of that same interval inverted, thus: from C to D two semitones,
and from D to C ten semitones — two and ten make "twelve." From C to E
four semitones, and from E to C eight semitones — four and eight make
"twelve."

TABLE OF THE INTERVALS AND OF THE INVERSIONS OF THE INTERVALS.

Name of the intervals.	Unison.	Second.	Third.	Fourth.	Fifth.	Sixth.	Seventh.	Octave.
Quality of the intervals.	perfect.	major.	major.	perfect.	perfect.	major.	major.	perfect.
Number of semitones in the intervals.	None.	2 semitones.	4 semitones.	5 semitones.	7 semitones.	9 semitones.	11 semitones.	12 semitones.
Intervals.								
Inversion of the intervals. Number of semitones in the intervals.	12 semitones.	10 semitones.	8 semitones.	7 semitones.	5 semitones.	3 semitones.	1 semitone.	None.
Quality of the intervals.	perfect.	minor.	minor.	perfect.	perfect.	minor.	minor.	perfect.
Name of the intervals.	Octave.	Seventh.	Sixth.	Fifth.	Fourth.	Third.	Second.	Unison.

EIGHTH CHAPTER.

—◆—

Phrasing.   PHRASING is the rendering or delivery of music.

Phrasing is the soul of music; it conveys to the hearer, in a clear and distinct manner, the thoughts and ideas contained in the music.

To phrase well, one must understand the rhythm, the measure, the members, phrases, sentences, and periods of music, and the cadences which are its punctuation; also the accent, which will be explained in the next chapter.

Rhythm.   Rhythm is an uneven division of time.

Rhythm expresses the relative length of duration or value of the notes, their particular accent, and the different movement or tempo of a piece.

It is this variety in the movement or tempo of a piece, in the value and accent of the notes, which gives to music a character of joy, sadness, animation, etc., and therefore, the rhythm is said to be lively, gay, or sad; in a word, the meaning of the music is contained in the rhythm. (See " Rhythm," page 13.)

Measure.   Measure is an even division of time. (See " Measure," page 40.)

Measure divides music into short portions of equal value, called bars, which are themselves subdivided into shorter portions of equal value, called beats. The time to be counted in a bar is the measure.

Difference between the measure and the rhythm.   The difference between the measure and the rhythm is such, that two pieces having the same measure will have an opposite character, according to their different rhythms.

Music is written in members, phrases, sentences, and periods.

Member.   A member is a part of a phrase, sentence, or period.

Phrase.   A phrase is a melodic or harmonic (See " Melody " and " Harmony," page 13,) succession of notes which conveys an idea.

Sentence.   A sentence is composed of one or more phrases, which conveys a complete idea, but does not end with a final cadence.

Period.   A period is a sentence ending with a final cadence.

Music is written in two forms or styles.   Music is written in two different forms: the " fugue " or " canonic," and the " metric " or " symmetric."

Fugue or Canonic form.   The fugue or canonic form is irregular in the length of its phrases, sentences, and periods, and may be compared to prose.

Metric or Symmetric form.   The metric or symmetric form is regular in the length of its phrases, sentences, and periods, and may be compared to verse.

In the most important works of the great masters, particularly so in J. S. Bach's, the fugue and metric forms are combined in the highest degree of perfection.

Music is generally written in the metric form; phrases, sentences, and periods of four, eight, or sixteen bars, are mostly used, then those of three or six bars, which sometimes are introduced in music written in phrases, sentences, or periods of four, eight, or sixteen bars. Phrases, sentences, or periods of five bars are rarely met with.

Cadences are the punctuation of music. Cadences.

Cadences divide music into phrases, sentences, and periods, and mark their members and conclusion.

A cadence is a repose, a fall, an end.

Cadences are indicated by a rest, a note of a longer value, or a chord.

A perfect or final cadence is on the perfect chord of the key-note, preceded by Perfect or final cadence the chord of the dominant,[1] both in the direct state. (See " Direct state of a Chord," page 52.)

Example :

An imperfect cadence is like a perfect or final one, but the perfect chord of Imperfect cadence. the key-note is not in the direct state.

Example :

The dominant chord not being in the direct state also renders the cadence more or less imperfect.

Examples :

or

A half cadence is on the chord of the dominant in the direct state. Half cadence.

Examples :

or

An interrupted or broken cadence is when the perfect or final cadence being Broken or interrupted cadence expected, a chord of any degree of the scale (generally the chord of the sixth degree,) or even a chord from another scale is substituted for the perfect chord of the key-note implied by the harmony. Examples : —

or   *or*   *or*

8   [1] See " One Word More," page 73.

Plagal cadence.   A plagal cadence is on the perfect chord of the key-note in the direct state, preceded by the chord of the sub-dominant in the direct state or not. A plagal cadence implies a conclusion, and is most generally used as an addition to the perfect or final one.

Examples : —

Fourth of a cadence.   A fourth of a cadence is the shortest of cadences. A rest, a note of a longer value, or a short member repeated, indicates a fourth of a cadence.

NINTH CHAPTER.

Accent.   IN music there are two kinds of accent : the " grammatical " or " primary," which is the lesser, and the " oratorical," which is the greater.

Grammatical accent.   The grammatical or primary accent belongs to each note in particular. It is the accent of the measure.

Oratorical accent.   The oratorical accent shades the whole phrase, sentence, or period, and marks the cadences. It is the accent of the phrasing.

GENERAL RULES FOR THE GRAMMATICAL ACCENT.

Measures of two beats make one trochee   Measures of two beats. 1 2
The first beat is strong, the second weak.

Measures of four beats make two trochees.   Measures of four beats .1 2 3 4
The first beat is strong, the third also, but in a lesser degree ; the second and fourth are weak.

Measures of eight beats.   Measures of eight beats. 1 2 3 4 5 6 7 8
Easier to count four beats twice 1 2 3 4 1 2 3 4
The first beat is strong, the fifth also, but in a lesser degree ; then the third and seventh ; the second and fourth, sixth and eighth are weak.

Measures of three beats make one dactyl.   Measures of three beats. 1 2 3
The first beat is strong, the second and third are weak.

Measures of six beats make two dactyls.   * Measures of six beats. 1 2 3 4 5 6
The first beat is strong, the fourth also, but in a lesser degree ; the second and third, fifth and sixth are weak.

* See page 59.

Measures of three quarter notes counted as six eighth notes 1 2 3 4 5 6

Measures of three quarter notes counted as six eighth notes make three trochees.

The first beat is strong, the third and fifth also, but in a lesser degree; the second, fourth and sixth are weak.

* Measures of six beats are sometimes to be accented in the same way; the rhythm will tell when to do so.

Measures of nine beats 1 2 3 4 5 6 7 8 9

Easier to count three times three 1 2 3 1 2 3 1 2 3

Measures of nine beats make three dactyls.

The first beat is strong, the fourth and the seventh also, but in a lesser degree; the second and third, fifth and sixth, eighth and ninth are weak.

Measures of twelve beats 1 2 3 4 5 6 7 8 9 10 11 12

Easier to count four times three 1 2 3 1 2 3 1 2 3 1 2 3

Measures of twelve beats make four dactyls.

The first beat is strong, the seventh also, but in a lesser degree; then the fourth and tenth; the second and third, fifth and sixth, eighth and ninth, eleventh and twelfth are weak.

1st. Never forget to mark the grammatical accent, particularly in difficult passages. Remarks.

2d. Do not neglect the weak accent; although weak, it is an accent.

3d. When the melody begins on the half of a beat, be particular not to accent the half, but the following beat, and thus prevent indecision.

4th. Be careful not to over-mark the grammatical accent.

SYNCOPE AND AGAINST TIME.

When the accent is on the weak beat of the measure or on the half of a beat, Syncope or Syncopation. if the value of the accented note _exceeds_ the value of the beat or of the half beat on which the accent falls, there is "syncopation," that is, a "syncope."

Examples: —

Accent on the weak beat of the measure.

Accent on the half beat.

When the accent is on the weak beat of the measure or on the half of a beat, Against time if the value of the accented note _does not exceed_ the value of the beat or of the half beat on which the accent falls, there is no syncopation, the accent is simply "against time."

Examples: —

Accent on the weak beat of the measure.

Accent on the half beat.

* See page 58.

GENERAL RULES FOR THE ORATORICAL ACCENT.

First. The oratorical accent claims " breathing."

" To breathe " when playing on the piano, is to take off the hands from the key-board, and to leave the pedal (if used.)

Sometimes one hand must breathe and the other not.

To know when and how long to breathe, is one of the greatest achievements of piano playing ; for at once the phrases, sentences and periods, their members and cadences, are made clear and distinct, and the phrasing or delivery of music perfect.

1st. If a cadence is perfect or final, a whole breathing is required.

2d. If the cadence is of less importance, a shorter breathing is taken.

3d. If a phrase is composed of several short members, a very short breathing after each member is necessary.

4th. Sometimes between phrases forming a sentence or period, or even in the middle of a phrase, a half breathing is advisable. A half breathing is to take off the hands and immediately keep on playing.

5th. When there is a rest, breathing is obligatory. (See " Rests," page 33.)

Second. The end of a phrase, sentence or period must always be softened, unless a crescendo, a f or a ff is marked, which makes an exception to this rule.

Third. When ascending, increase the tone, that is, play louder ; when descending, decrease the tone.

Fourth. When the member of a phrase, or a phrase, is repeated several times in succession, each time the tone must increase, as : loud, louder, loudest. Sometimes the very opposite is required.

Fifth. When there is a slur over two notes of different name, the first one is always accented and both notes must be played very legato. Two such notes are like a word of two syllables, as : " mūsic." (A slur over two notes of the same name has no reference to accent, but simply makes the second note tied. See " Note tied," page 35.)

Sixth. The harmony always follows the shading of the melody, but in a lesser degree, so that the melody may be distinctly heard.

Seventh. If one hand has a melody and also some other notes to play, particular care must be taken that the melody is distinctly heard above the other notes.

Eighth. When the original theme (air or melody) returns, it should be preceded by a " ritard ; " but exact time must be resumed on the very first note of said theme.

Ninth. An f marked in a soft passage is sometimes, but not generally, meant to be as loud as that marked in a loud one, but is only so in comparison with the rest of the passage ; in like manner a p marked in a loud passage is to be played comparatively soft. (This rule is not applicable when a contrast is wanted.)

Tenth. Whenever the rules of the grammatical and oratorical accent conflict, the oratorical or greater accent overrules the grammatical or lesser one; as for instance, when the end of a phrase, sentence or period (which must always be softened) falls on the first beat of a bar, (which beat is always strong.)

To hold back a note is to wait an instant longer than the proper time before playing it, so that it is desired by the ear. Exact time is kept, but not on that particular note. *A note held back.*

The note or notes are somewhat hurried for a particular purpose, for instance to express anxiety. *A note or notes played somewhat too soon.*

To " ritard " is to diminish the speed by degrees. A ritard, to have its full effect, must not be begun too soon, and exact time must be resumed the very instant the ritard is over. *Ritard.*

A pause generally is preceded by a ritard, and indicates to hold the note over which it is placed longer than its real value. Its effect is grand and noble. *Pause.*

The word " Crescendo " or simply " Cres," or this sign ⎯⎯⎯⎯ indicates to increase the tone gradually. *Crescendo.*

The word " Decrescendo " or simply " Decres," or this sign ⎯⎯⎯⎯ indicates to decrease the tone gradually. *Decrescendo.*

1st. Do not let your playing be monotonous; shade perfectly the crescendos and decrescendos; break the sameness by well marking the accent and the contrasts, that is, the sudden loud and soft, the gay and sad passages, etc. *Remarks*

2d. Let music have its full effect, by playing a pianissimo truly soft and a fortissimo truly loud.

3d. When a passage is to be shaded from soft to the loudest tone the piano can give, never stop increasing until the whole power of the piano is brought out, else the effect of the passage is lost.

4th. The same rule applies to the opposite shade.

Note.—Any exception to these General Rules will be learned only in meeting with the different cases.

PART OF ANDANTE FROM BEETHOVEN'S SONATA OP. 26. (Apply all the rules mentioned in the preceding chapters; also pay attention to every sign, word, etc.)

* See " Trill," page 76. † † These two chords fill the harmony and lead to the repetition of the Theme.

TENTH CHAPTER.

—◆—

Scales. THEORETICALLY there are twenty-four major and twenty-four minor scales; practically there are but twelve of each. The others, with a few exceptions, are never used.

NAMES OF THE SCALES.

Major scales.	Minor scales.
C.	A.
G.	E.
D.	B.
A.	F♯.
E.	C♯.
B.	G♯.
F♯ or G♭.	D♯ or E♭.
C♯ or D♭.	A♯ or B♭.
A♭.	F.
E♭.	C.
B♭.	G.
F.	D.

Order of the scales with sharps.* The scales with sharps are found in order, every perfect fifth in ascending and every perfect fourth in descending.

Order of the sharps. The sharps themselves are found in the same order, that is: every perfect fifth in ascending and every perfect fourth in descending.

The note which is a perfect fifth above another note, is also a perfect fourth below that same note. Example: G is a perfect fifth above and a perfect fourth below C. Thus:

Order of the scales with flats.† The scales with flats are found in order, every perfect fourth in ascending and every perfect fifth in descending.

Order of the flats. The flats themselves are found in the same order, that is: every perfect fourth in ascending and every perfect fifth in descending.

The note which is a perfect fourth above another note, is also a perfect fifth below that same note. Example: F is a perfect fourth above and a perfect fifth below C. Thus:

* See "Why the scales with sharps and the sharps are found in the order," etc., page 63.
† See "Why the scales with flats and the flats are found in the order," etc., page 64.

The scale of " G " is the first scale with sharps. It is the one most similar to Scales with sharps. the scale of " C," its intervals being exactly the same with one exception, the seventh, which is minor instead of major. (From G to F, seven notes and ten semitones, minor seventh.) A minor seventh is a wrong interval in a major scale and brings with itself another fault, the absence of the leading-note. (See " Leading-note," page 50.) The leading-note must be a major seventh, that is, seven notes and eleven semitones above the key-note. Without a leading-note there is no key, consequently the minor seventh must be rendered major. By raising the seventh degree one semitone we have a new note, the first sharp " F," which adds one semitone to the seventh and renders it major, (from G to F♯, seven notes and eleven semitones, major seventh,) the leading-note at once is in its proper place: F♯ is seven notes and eleven semitones above the key-note " G," naturally is also one semitone below the " G " octave of the key-note, since there are twelve semitones in an octave.

The same difficulty about the minor seventh is met with in every one of the major scales with sharps, and the same rule must be applied.

Every scale brings in a new sharp which is its leading-note, and becomes one Important to remember. of the real notes of the following scale.

The scale of " D " is the second scale with sharps, because after G it is the one Why the scales with sharps and the sharps are found in the order mentioned, page 62. whose intervals are most like those of the scale of C. The scale of " A " is the third scale with sharps, because after D it is the one whose intervals are most like those of the scale of C, etc. Every new major scale with sharps is a perfect fifth above and at the same time a perfect fourth below the scale which precedes it ; the seventh degree of the scale, which being raised one semitone became the first sharp, varies just as the key-note does. From this comes the rule that the scales with sharps and the sharps are found in order, every perfect fifth in ascending and every perfect fourth in descending.

To find the key in which the music is written with sharps at the signature, Rule to find the key in which the music is written with sharps at the signature. remember that the seventh degree of the scale is made sharp (by raising it one semitone) to render the seventh " major " and have a " leading-note."

RULE. — *The last sharp is the leading-note of the key in which the music is written.*

Example :

Two sharps at the signature " F " and " C," the last sharp is C, leading-note of " D." The music is written in the key of D major.

Explanation. The key-note is one semitone above the leading-note; in the above example the leading-note is C♯, one semitone above it, is D : " D " is the key-note.

WITH THE FOLLOWING NUMBER OF SHARPS AT THE SIGNATURE, WHAT IS THE KEY ?

Scales with
flats.
The scale of "F" is the first scale with flats. It is the one most similar to the scale of "C," its intervals being exactly the same with one exception, the fourth, which is augmented instead of perfect. (From F to B, four notes and six semitones, augmented fourth.) An augmented fourth is a wrong interval in a major scale, consequently that augmented fourth must be rendered perfect. By lowering the fourth degree one semitone, we have a new note, the first flat "B," which takes off one semitone from the fourth and renders it perfect. (From F to B♭, four notes and five semitones, perfect fourth.)

The same difficulty about the augmented fourth is met with in every one of the major scales with flats, and the same rule must be applied.

Important to
remember.
Every scale brings in a new flat which is a perfect fourth above its key-note, and becomes one of the real notes of the following scale.

Why the scales
with flats and
the flats are
found in the
order men-
tioned, page 62.
The scale of "B♭" is the second scale with flats, because after F it is the one whose intervals are most like those of the scale of C. The scale of "E♭" is the third scale with flats, because after B♭ it is the one whose intervals are most like those of the scale of C, etc. Every new major scale with flats is a perfect fourth above and at the same time a perfect fifth below the scale which precedes it; the fourth degree of the scale, which being lowered one semitone became the first flat, varies just as the key-note does. From this comes the rule that the scales with flats and the flats are found in order, every perfect fourth in ascending and every perfect fifth in descending.

Rule to find
the key in
which the mu-
sic is written
with flats at
the signature.
To find the key in which the music is written with flats at the signature, remember that the fourth degree of the scale is made flat (by lowering it one semitone) to render the fourth "perfect."

RULE. — *A perfect fourth below the last flat is the key-note of the key in which the music is written.* (Since the flats are found in order, every perfect fourth in ascending, it follows that the last but one is always the key-note.)

Example :

Two flats at the signature "B" and "E," the last flat is E, a perfect fourth below it, is B♭: "B♭" is the key-note. The music is written in the key of B♭ major.

IN WHAT KEY ARE WRITTEN THE FOLLOWING EXAMPLES?

NOTE. — These examples are taken from four sonatas of Mozart.

ELEVENTH CHAPTER.

ELEVENTH CHAPTER.

In music there are two modes : the " major" and the " minor." *Mode.*
Mode specifies a particular state of the diatonic scale, and is determined by the
places of the semitones.

The third, sixth, and seventh degrees of a diatonic scale are called " modal *Modal notes.*
notes," because by being raised or lowered they change the quality of the third,
sixth, and seventh intervals, and therefore determine the mode.

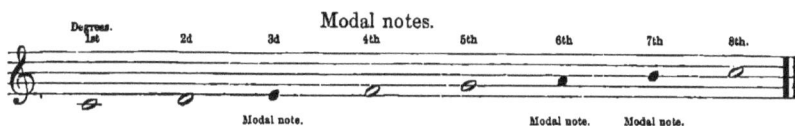

In the major mode the third, the sixth, and the seventh intervals are major, *Major mode.*
the semitones are placed from the third degree to the fourth, and from the
seventh to the eighth ; so that a major scale always progresses in the following
order : first, " two tones," then " one semitone," next " three tones," lastly " one
semitone."

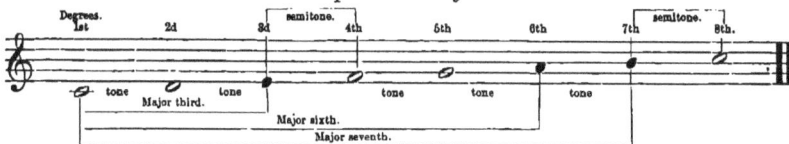

In the minor mode, the third, the sixth and the seventh intervals are minor, *Minor mode.*
the semitones are placed from the second degree to the third, and from the fifth
to the sixth ; so that a minor scale *ought* to progress in the following order :
first " one tone," then " one semitone," next " two tones," then " one semitone,"
lastly " two tones."

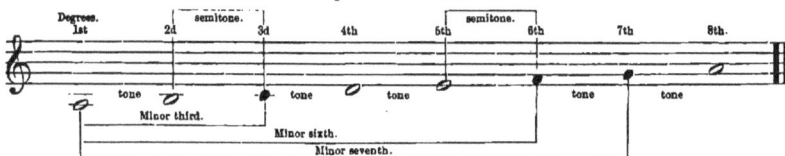

This is the minor scale as it ought to be; this is the true minor scale in its
entire character of minor ; but if the seventh interval is minor, there is no
leading-note, and without a leading-note there is no key ; hence, the impossibility

Melodic minor scale, first minor scale. of preserving the minor seventh, and consequently this interval is made major; *one modal note is now destroyed.* If the seventh is major and the sixth remains minor, there is an interval of a tone and a half between the minor sixth and the major seventh; such an interval is forbidden in the diatonic order, which progresses by intervals of tones and semitones; therefore this interval is also made major, and *two modal notes are now destroyed.* The leading-note, so called because it leads to the key-note, has not the same influence in descending the scale; therefore, in descending, the minor seventh is restored to the scale, the sixth naturally follows the seventh and becomes again minor, so that in descending, the scale stands in its entire character of minor; the three modal notes are there, but there is no longer a leading-note.

Résumé of the melodic minor scale. In ascending, the third is minor, the sixth and the seventh are major; in descending, those three intervals are minor. The semitones are placed from the second degree to the third, and from the seventh to the eighth, in ascending the scale; in descending they are placed from the sixth degree to the fifth, and from the third to the second; so that the first or melodic minor scale progresses in the following order: —

Ascending — First "one tone," then "one semitone," next "four tones," lastly "one semitone."

Descending — First "two tones," then "one semitone," next "two tones," then "one semitone," lastly "one tone."

Example of the melodic minor scale in "A minor."

This is the first minor scale, called the melodic minor scale because it progresses by intervals of tones and semitones, intervals whose intonation is easy for the voice; consequently this minor scale is the best for melody.

One modal note in ascending the scale and no leading-note in descending were *Harmonic minor scale, second minor scale.* not always satisfactory. Therefore a second minor scale was made, which preserves two of the modal notes, the third and the sixth, and the leading-note, both in ascending and descending the scale; but an augmented second, the forbidden interval of a tone and a half, is there between the minor sixth and the major seventh.

Résumé of the harmonic minor scale. Both in ascending and descending, the third and the sixth are minor and the seventh major. The semitones are placed from the second degree to the third, from the fifth to the sixth, and from the seventh to the eighth; so that the second or harmonic minor scale progresses in the following order: first "one tone," then "one semitone," next "two tones," then "one semitone," next "the forbidden interval of a tone and a half," (which makes an augmented second from the sixth to the seventh degree of the scale,) lastly "one semitone."

Example of the harmonic minor scale in " A minor."

This is the second minor scale, called the harmonic minor scale, because both in ascending and descending it has a leading-note and two of the modal notes, therefore has in itself more of the character of a minor scale, consequently is the best for harmony.

The " melodic " minor scale in ascending has one modal note only, the " third ; " in descending has the three modal notes, but no leading-note. *Résumé of both melodic and harmonic minor scales.*

The " harmonic " minor scale in ascending and descending has a leading-note, two of the modal notes, and an interval of augmented second from the sixth degree to the seventh.

The above explanations prove it an impossibility to have a minor scale in its *Conclusion.* integral character of minor, for the minor scale with the three modal notes in *First.* ascending and descending is inadmissible because there is no leading-note.

The first or melodic minor scale with the sixth and the seventh major in *Second.* ascending and minor in descending has the three following objections : —

1st — It loses in ascending two of the modal notes, which makes the second half of the scale " major."

Example in " A minor."

2d — In descending there is no leading-note, and therefore, in descending, the scale has all the notes constituting a major scale, thus : —

Example in " A minor."   It gives all the notes constituting " C major."

3d — In descending, the scale produces two chromatic semitones with the ascending scale, which brings the chromatic order into that scale, *without* breaking the diatonic order.

Example in " A minor."

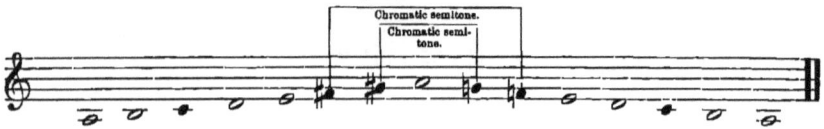

Third. The second or harmonic minor scale with the minor sixth and the major seventh, both in ascending and descending, has the two following objections : —
1st — It loses one of the modal notes, both in ascending and descending.

Example in " A minor."

2d — There is an augmented second composed of a tone and of a chromatic semitone, between the minor sixth and the major seventh : such an interval is difficult of intonation, and brings the chromatic order into the scale, *breaking* the diatonic order.

Example in " A minor."

How to distinguish the major mode from the minor one. Remark that in either of the two minor scales, the " third " is the only modal note which always remains ; therefore, to ascertain the mode of a scale or of a chord, the surest rule is the " third," thus : —

RULE.— *If the third is major, the mode is major ; if the third is minor, the mode is minor.*

Examples : —

Perfect chord of C major.

Perfect chord of A minor.

WHY A NOTE IS MADE DOUBLE SHARP OR DOUBLE FLAT, INSTEAD OF BEING
CALLED BY THE NAME OF THE KEY ON WHICH IT IS PLAYED.

Note. — Play all the examples on the piano and verify them while reading on.

Notes are made double sharp to render the intervals either major or aug- Why there are double sharps.
mented ; also to have a leading-note.

EXAMPLE of a note made double sharp, to render a minor interval major, and have a leading-note.

The scale of " G sharp minor " is the first one with a double sharp, and progresses thus : —   G ♯, A ♯, B, C ♯, D ♯, E, F ✗, G ♯.

(F double sharp being played on the key called " G.")

From the key-note of a scale to its seventh degree, there must be a major
seventh, that is, seven notes and eleven semitones. If F double sharp is called
" G," it makes eight notes instead of seven ; and if " F sharp " is played, there are
ten semitones instead of eleven. Therefore it must be *F double sharp* played on
the key called " G."

Besides, the leading-note must be the note preceding the key-note, therefore in
the scale of G sharp minor, it must be an " F ; " and as the leading-note must be
a semitone below the key-note, it follows that in the scale of G sharp minor it
must be an *F double sharp.*

Moreover if F double sharp was called " G," that scale would progress thus : —

G ♯, A ♯, B, C ♯, D ♯, E, " G," G ♯

Two G's, one sharp and one natural, and no F, — such a scale is impossible.

EXAMPLE of a note made double sharp to render a major interval augmented.

From D to F ♯ there are three notes and four semitones, which make a *major
third ;* to render that interval augmented the F sharp must be made. double
sharp ; and thus, from D to F ✗ there are three notes and five semitones, which
make an *augmented third.*

EXAMPLE of a note made double sharp to render a perfect interval augmented.

From F ♯ to C ♯ there are five notes and seven semitones, which make a *perfect fifth ;* to render that interval augmented the C sharp must be made double
sharp ; and thus from F ♯ to C ✗ there are five notes and eight semitones, which
make an *augmented fifth.*

Notes are made double flat to render the intervals minor or diminished. Why there are double flats.

EXAMPLE of a note made double flat to render a major interval minor.

From G ♭ to B ♭ there are three notes and four semitones, which make a
major third ; to render that interval minor, the B flat must be made double flat ;
and thus from G ♭ to B ♭♭ there are three notes and three semitones, which
make a *minor third.*

EXAMPLE of a note made double flat to render a perfect interval diminished.

From A ♭ to E ♭ there are five notes and seven semitones, which make a *perfect fifth ;* to render that interval diminished, the E flat must be made double
flat ; and thus from A ♭ to E ♭♭ there are five notes and six semitones, which
make a *diminished fifth.*

Major Scales.   **Melodic Minor Scales.**   **Harmonic Minor Scales.**

Note. — The want of room obliges us to have the scales of one octave only; but one note over the octave is written with the proper fingering to continue the scale to two or more octaves.

C major, Signature? None.   A minor, Signature? None.   A minor, Signature? None.

G major, Signature? One sharp, F.   E minor, Signature? One sharp, F.   E minor, Signature? One sharp, F

D major, Signature? Two sharps, F, C.   D minor, Signature? Two sharps, F, C.   B minor, Signature? Two sharps, F, C.

A major, Signature? Three sharps, F, C, G.   F sharp minor, Signature? Three sharps, F, C, G.   F sharp minor, Signature? Three sharps, F, C, G.

E major, Signature? Four sharps, F, C, G, D.   C sharp minor, Signature? Four sharps, F, C, G, D.   C sharp minor, Signature? Four sharps, F, C, G, D

B major, Signature? Five sharps, F, C, G, D, A.   G sharp minor, Signature? Five sharps, F, C, G, D, A.   G sharp minor, Signature? Five sharps, F, C, G, D,

arp major, Signature? Six sharps, F, C, G, D, A, E.   D sharp minor, Signature? Six sharps, F, C, G, D, A, E.   D sharp minor, Signature? Six sharps, F, C, G, D, A, E.

flat major, Signature? Five flats, D, E, A, D, G.   D flat minor, Signature? Five flats, B, E, A, D, G.   D flat minor, Signature? Five flats, D, E, A, D, G.

A flat major, Signature? Four flats, D, E, A, D.   F minor, Signature? Four flats, B, E, A, D.   F minor, Signature? Four flats, D, E, A, D.

E flat major, Signature? Three flats, B, E, A.   C minor, Signature? Three flats, B, E, A.   C minor, Signature? Three flats, B, E, A.

B flat major, Signature? Two flats, B, E.   G minor, Signature? Two flats, B, E.   G minor, Signature? Two flats, B, E.

F major, Signature? One flat, B.   D minor, Signature? One flat, B.   D minor, Signature? One flat, B.

TWELFTH CHAPTER.

Relative or kindred keys.   KEYS are relative or kindred, when their signature is the same, or when the difference between their signatures is but one accident, be it one more or one less.

Relative or kindred keys of major scales.   Every major scale has *five* relative or kindred keys.

1st — *Its own minor relative,* which is a minor third below the key-note of the major key, being also a major sixth above that key-note.

Example in C major.

2d — *Two major relatives,* which are respectively a perfect fifth above and a perfect fifth below the key-note of the major key.

Example in C major.

The note which is a perfect fifth above a key-note is the fifth degree of the scale, the " dominant; " the note which is a perfect fifth below a key-note is also a perfect fourth above that key-note, and is the fourth degree of the scale, the " sub-dominant; " therefore the sub-dominant and the dominant of a major key are always the key-notes of the major relatives of that key.

3d — *The minor relatives* of the two major relatives.

Example in C major. — C is the key-note.

Remark.   A major key and its minor relative have always the same signature.

How to find whether the music is written in the major key or in its minor relative.   To find whether the music is written in the major key or in its minor relative, the first and best rule is the following one.

1st Rule : Sing the first phrase or so mentally, in order to understand its musical sense ; if the cadence is on the perfect chord of the major key or of its dominant, the music is written in the major key ; but if the cadence is on the

* † ‡ The minor keys having either of these marks are the minor relatives of the major keys having the same marks.

perfect chord of the minor relative or of its dominant, the music is written in the minor relative.

To find the chord in any particular position is not necessary : in addition to the positions belonging to a chord its constituting notes may be found in very many different positions.

Examples : —

Some of the notes of the chord may even be omitted, as in the first and fifth examples. A little practice will soon teach how to distinguish a chord.

2d Rule : Never forget that the leading-note of the minor relative does not belong to the signature, but comes in as an accidental accident, so that if the perfect chord of the major key or of its dominant is found in the first few bars of the music, the music is written in the major key ; but if the perfect chord of the minor relative is found in the first few bars of the music and the fifth degree of the major key (which becomes the leading-note of the minor relative,) is altered, so as to be the accidental accident leading-note of the minor relative, the music is written in the minor relative.

Sometimes the music *is not* written in the minor relative, although its leading-note is found in the first few bars of the music ; because it is there simply as a melodic ornament, (See " Melodic Ornaments," page 75,) and therefore does not affect the key-note. *Exceptions. 1st.*

Sometimes, on the contrary, the music *is* written in the minor relative, although its leading-note is not found in the first few bars of the music ; because the leading-note itself perhaps does not occur for some length of time, or being there it has not the proper alteration at once, being considered to belong to the descending melodic minor scale. (See page 66.) *2d.*

3d Rule : Music as a general rule ends in the same key as that in which it begins.

It is said in the Sixth Chapter, that a chord of three notes can be built on every one of the degrees of the scale ; if a fourth note, a minor seventh from the fundamental, is added to the chord built on the " dominant" fifth degree of the scale, the chord of dominant-seventh is formed. *One word more. Chord of dominant-seventh*

Example :

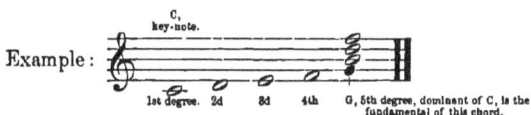

C, key-note.

1st degree. 2d 3d 4th G, 5th degree, dominant of C, is the fundamental of this chord.

The chord of dominant-seventh takes its name both from its fundamental and its upper degree, and has four positions, thus: —

Positions of the dominant-seventh chord.

G dominant of C, is the
fundamental of this chord.

Natural resolution of the dominant-seventh chord. The chord of dominant-seventh has its natural resolution (See " Resolution," in *Musical Dictionary*) on the perfect chord of the key-note, the leading-note of which, being the third of the dominant-seventh chord, naturally ascends to the key-note.

Examples: —

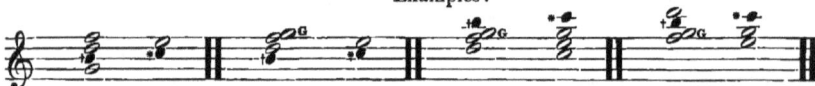

G fundamental.
† B leading-note.
* C key-note.

Difference between the dominant chord and the dominant-seventh chord. When the chord built on the fifth degree of a scale or key is composed of *three notes*, it is the dominant chord of that scale or key; when composed of *four notes*, it is the dominant-seventh chord of that scale or key.

Dominant chord of
C major.

G, dominant of C, is the
fundamental of this chord.

Examples : —

Dominant-seventh
chord of C major.

G, dominant of C, is the
fundamental of this chord.

Remark. Be careful, when looking at music, to analyze the chords, so as to distinguish those that belong to the key from those that do not.

Example : —

1. Perfect chord of " C major," first position.
2.   "   "   "   "   second position.
3.   "   "   "   "   third position.
4. Dominant seventh chord of " C major," first position.
5. Perfect chord of " C major," third position.
* 6. Dominant chord of " C major," first position.
† 7.   "   "   "   "   second position.

8. Dominant seventh chord of " G major," fourth position.
9. Dominant chord of " G major," first position.
† 10. Perfect chord of " G major," second position (inverted.)
* 11. " " " " first position, etc.

NOTE. — Compare the two chords marked thus : * ; also the two marked thus : †

MELODIC ORNAMENTS.

MELODIC ornaments are written in small notes or expressed by a sign placed *Melodic ornaments.*
over the notes. They *do not* belong to the harmony, and for this reason are only
melodic accidental notes ; but Harmonic accidental notes are so called because
they *do* belong to the harmony. (See " Suspensions," in *Musical Dictionary*.) In
music there are four principal melodic ornaments, namely : the " appoggiature,"
the " mordant," the " group," and the " trill."

The note by which a " melodic ornament " is placed, or over which is placed *Principal note.*
the " sign " of a melodic ornament, is called *principal note*, and is the note to which
the melodic ornament belongs.

The principal note is a note of the piece and has a real value in the measure,
while the note or notes of the melodic ornament (being only ornaments,) have
no real value in the measure, but take more or less of the value of the principal
note.

There is no rule to tell exactly how much of the value of the principal note a
melodic ornament takes ; it varies according to circumstances. The rhythm of
the music, taste and experience are the surest guides.

The appoggiature is either single or double, and is composed of one or two *Appoggiature.*
small notes placed before the principal note.

Examples : —

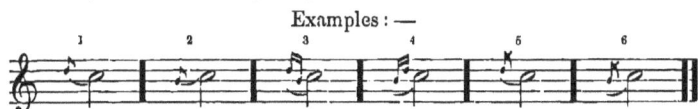

A bar across the appoggiature, as in the fifth and sixth examples, indicates
that it should be played very short, the accent falling on the principal note
which is struck at the exact time. In the other examples, the appoggiature
takes some of the value of the principal note.

Mordant means *bite the note.* The mordant is composed of two small notes *Mordant.*
placed before the principal note. The first one of the small notes is like the
principal note ; the second is either the note above or the note below it, most
generally the note above it.

Examples :

Very often it is expressed by a sign placed over the note.

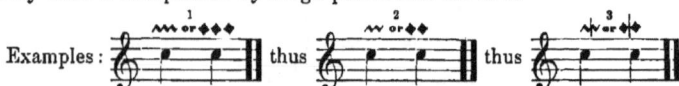

Examples: thus   thus

A bar across the mordant, as in the third example, indicates that it should be played very quickly, the accent falling on the principal note, which is struck at the exact time.

The mordant expressed as in the second example is the one most generally met with; it takes a little of the value of the principal note, but is played so quickly that the principal note almost comes in time. The accent falls on the first note of the mordant.

Remark. The bar across the mordant is often neglected, so that quite frequently the mordant expressed thus: ∿ (second example) should be played as the one expressed thus: ∿ (third example.)

The mordant expressed as in the first example is played rather slowly and takes some of the value of the principal note. It also sometimes implies a slow trill.

Group or Turn. The group or turn is composed of three or four small notes, preceding or following the principal note; most generally these: the principal note, (played or not like a small note according to what the music demands,) then the note above it, the principal note again, then the note below it, and finally the principal note; then what is written on the music.   Examples: —

The seventh and eleventh examples are most generally used.

Very often it is expressed by this sign ∾ placed over the note.

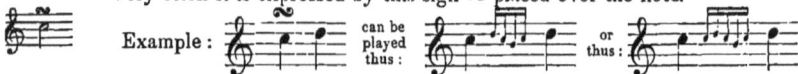

Example: can be played thus: or thus:

A sharp, a flat, or a natural, placed over or under, or both over and under the sign of the group, indicates that the note over or under the principal note is either sharp, flat, or natural.   Examples: —

A bar across the group thus: ∾ indicates that it should be played very quickly.

Trill. The trill is expressed by the two letters " *tr* " placed over the principal note.

Thus:

To trill is to repeat alternately, rapidly and without interruption, the principal note and the note above it.

The principal note and the note above it are repeated four times over for a General rule. quarter note, however the movement or tempo of the music may vary this rule.

The trill must be begun on the principal note; if begun on any other note but the principal one, it is a "false trill."

Example: [musical notation] is to be played thus :—

[musical notation]

After the trill is finished, a group or turn (always beginning with the principal End of the trill. note,) is added to it as a complete ending; without an ending the trill is not perfect, except when the trill itself does not allow an ending.

The end of the trill has an accent on its first note, is played faster than the trill itself, and takes some of the value of the last beat of the trill.

Examples :—

[musical notation] is to be played thus :—

[musical notation] is to be played thus :

[musical notation] is to be played thus :

or thus : [musical notation]

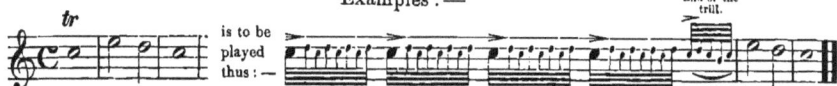

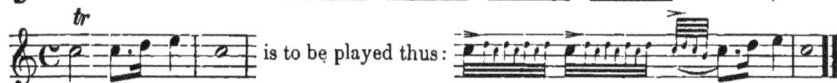

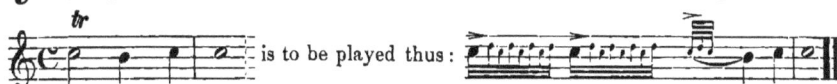

A group or part of a group is sometimes written after the trill, but whether Remarks. expressed or not, to add it (when allowable,) makes a more perfect finish to the 1. trill.

Example *where the music does not allow an ending :*

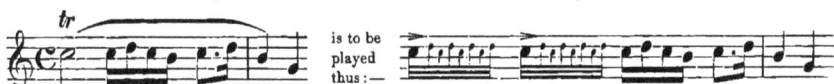

[musical notation] is to be played thus :—

If "*tr*" is written in a passage too rapid to allow of a trill, a group is played 2. instead.

In such a passage as this : [musical notation] the trill is kept on from 3. one note to the other without interruption, adding or not the end of the trill after each note, according to what the music demands.

TRANSPOSITION.

Transposition. To transpose is to write or play in a different key from the one written, by raising or lowering every note of any given interval.

Transposition is principally used to bring a song into the key most favorable for the voice.

Example in A major: —

ENFANTS, N'Y TOUCHEZ PAS.

Paroles de H. Guérin.

Musique de Clapisson.

riten.

sempre dolce.

las! pourquoi faire ain - si le tourment? Ce nid, ce doux mystè-re, Que

a tempo.

colla voce.

animato. *poco a poco.*

vous guettez d'en bas, C'est l'espoir du printemps, c'est l'amour d'une mère! ——

animato. *poco a poco.*

sentito. *f* *rall e espress.*

Enfants, n'y touchez pas! Enfants, n'y touchez pas!

pp

a tempo. *tr*

rall. *pp sempre.* *graziosetto.*

tr

rit.

The same transposed in A♭ major.

Note. — Rather than to repeat the same verse in the transpositions of this song, the second and third verses are adopted as more agreeable ; but the changes of the words require the melody to vary in some places.

Qui chan-te - ra Dieu, la brise et les ro - ses, Mé - chants, si vous tu - ez ces jeunes voix é - clo - ses ? Qui chan-te - ra Dieu la brise et les ro - ses ?

dolcissimo. *riten.* *sempre dolce.*

Au-tour de vous   tout s'en at-tris - te- ra.   Ce - nid,—   ce doux mystè-re, que

a tempo.

colla voce.

animato   *poco a poco.*

vous guettez d'en bas,   C'est l'espoir du prin-temps,   c'est l'amour d'u-ne mère ! —

animato   *poco a poco.*

sentito. **f** *rit.* *rall e espress.*

Enfants, n'y touchez pas ! En-fants, n'y touchez pas !

pp

a tempo. *tr*

rall. *pp sempre.* *graziosetto.*

tr

rit.

The same transposed in G major. (See "Note," page 80.)

Allegretto. ♩ = 80.
graziosetto.
dolce sempre.

riten. *silence.*

Slower.
simplice e sotto voce.

Dieu seul a droit sur tout ce qui res - pi - re, Ne pouvant rien cré - er il

pp

ne faut rien dé-trui - re, Dieu seul a droit, sur tout ce qui res - pi - re,

Beaux marau-deurs, prenez garde, Il vous voit. Ce nid, — ce doux mystè-re, que

vous guettez d'en bas, C'est l'espoir du printemps, C'est l'amour d'une mère! —

Enfants, n'y touchez pas! Enfants—n'y touchez pas !

ACCENTED EXERCISES.

Note. — See the last paragraph of the Introduction.

Play all the notes like quarter notes, very slow and firm, then faster by degrees.   (The half notes
are used only to render the accented notes more prominent.)

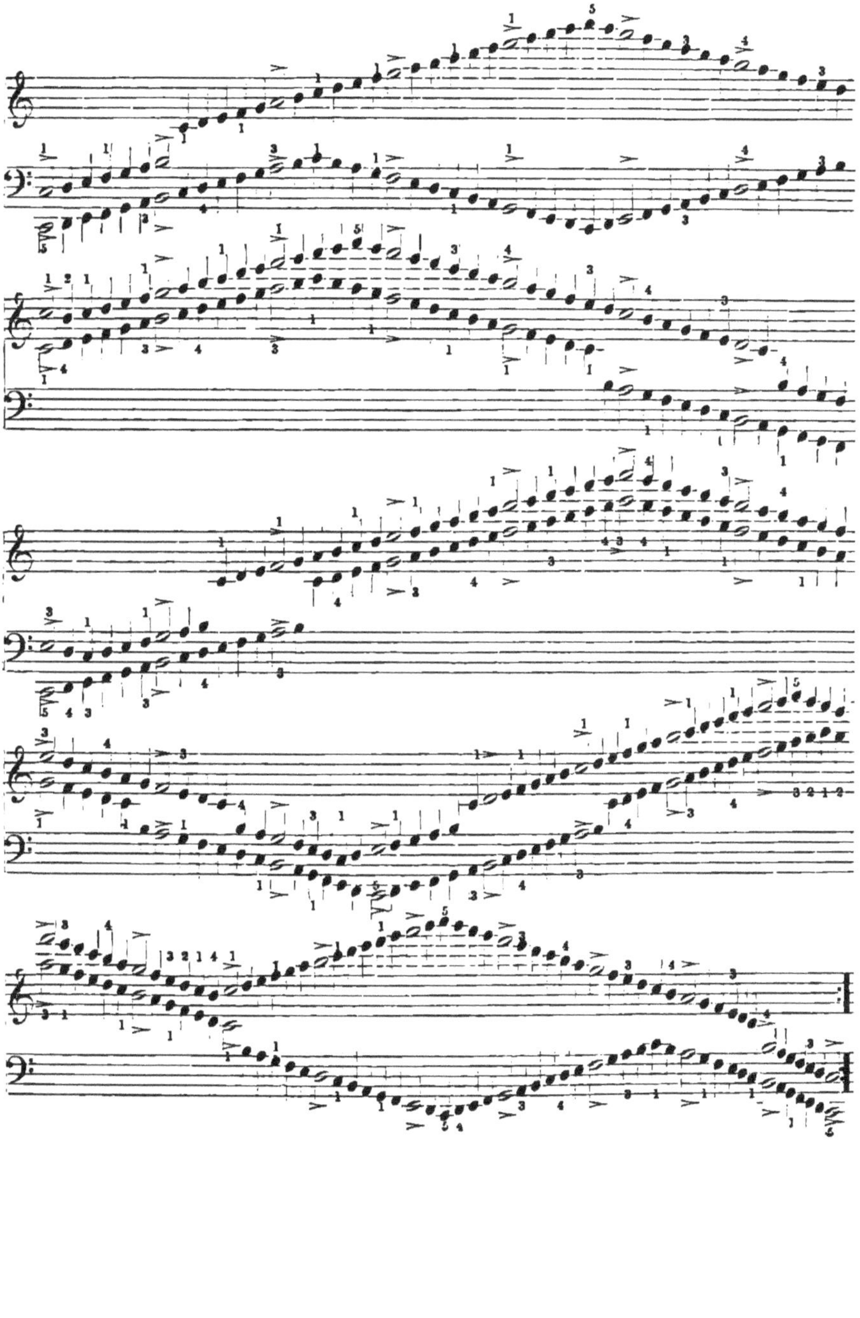

OCTAVES EXERCISES.

Note. — See " How to play Octaves and Chords," page 20.

SIXTHS EXERCISES.

When out of practice, the playing of the following exercises for ten minutes will render the fingers remarkably tractable.

Slow and Legato.

Note. — In the following three pages, the accidental accidents alter only the notes before which they are placed; this is an exception to the rule. (See "Accidental Accident," page 40.)

Règle d'Octave in the three positions.

The Règle d'Octave, also called "Harmonic Scale," is an harmonic form which has the ascending and descending major or minor scale for a bass, and assigns to each degree one particular chord which belongs invariably to it.

1st position.   C MAJOR.

2d position.

3d position.

1st position.   A MINOR.

2d position.

3d position.

From C major............to........................D flat major; returns to...........C major.

From C major........................to..................D major; returns to...........C major.

From C major..............to ....E flat major; returns to............C major.

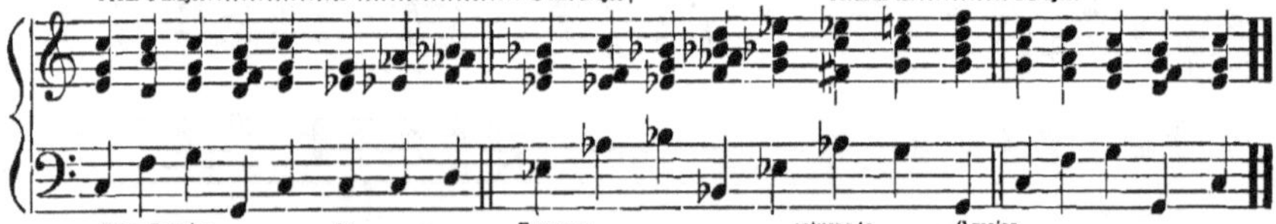

From C major..............to...................E major; returns to.........C major.

From C major........................to........F major; returns to............C major.

From C major.........to..............................G flat major; returns to..................C major.

From C major.........................to........................G major; returns to C major.

From C major............to.....................A flat major ;   returns to.............C major.

From C major.............to.....................A major ;   returns to.............C major

From C major.............to...................B flat major ;   returns to...................C major.

From C major.............to.....................D major ;   returns to.............C major.

SHORTER FORMS OF MODULATION.

C....to....D flat.   C......to........D.   C....to.....E flat.   C.....to..........E.   C...to..F.   C.............to................G flat.

C........to.........G.   C......to.......A flat.   C........to..........A.   C....to...B flat.   C.............to..............B.

PIANO COMPOSITIONS MOST USEFUL IN A PRIVATE MUSICAL LIBRARY.

Symphonies for two or four hands: Haydn, Mozart, Beethoven.

The study of symphonies is very advantageous; it also enables one to understand and appreciate them better when performed by the orchestra.

Sonatas: Haydn, Mozart, Beethoven.

(Mozart's sonatas for four hands are particularly attractive.) Haydn and Mozart have not arranged their sonatas in any particular order. They have been published by several houses in different orders.

Beethoven arranged his sonatas in the following order:—

1. *Op. 2. No. 1. F minor.*
Allegro. (♩ — 108.)

2. *Op. 2. No. 2. A major.*
Allegro vivace. (♩ — 144.)

3. *Op. 2. No. 3. C major.*
Allegro con brio. (♩ — 76.)

4. *Op. 7. E♭ major.*
Allo. molto con brio. (♩ — 116.)

5. *Op. 10. No. 1. C minor.*
Allo. con spirito. (♩ — 76.)

6. *Op. 10. No 2. F major.*
Allegro. (♩ — 96.)

7. *Op. 10. No. 3. D major.*
Presto. (♩ — 132.)

8. *Op. 13. C minor.* (Pathetic.)
Grave. (♪ — 60.)

9. *Op. 14. No. 1. E major.*
Allegro. (♩ — 152.)

10. *Op. 14. No. 2. G major*
Allegro. (♪ — 160.)

11. *Op. 22. B♭ major.*
Allegro con brio. (♩ — 84.)

12. *Op. 26. A♭ major.*
Andante. (♪ — 80.)

13. *Op. 27. No. 1. E♭ major.*
Andante (♩ — 76.)

14. *Op. 27. No. 2. C♯ minor.*
(Moonlight sonata.)
Adagio sost. (♩ — 60.)

15. *Op. 28. D major.*
Allegro. (♩ — 60.)

16. *Op. 31. No. 1. G major.*
Allegro. vivace. (♩ — 160.)

17. *Op. 31. No. 2. D minor.*
Largo. (♩ — 50.)   Allo. (♩ 126)

18. *Op 31. No. 3. E♭ major.*
Allegro. (♩ — 160.)

19. *Op. 49. No. 1. G minor.*
Andante. (♩ — 69.)

20. *Op. 49. No. 2. G major.*
Allo. ma non troppo. (♩ — 160.)

21. *Op. 53. C major.*
Allo. con brio. (♩ — 88.)

22. *Op. 54. F major.*
Tempo di Minuetto. (♩ — 120.)

23. *Op. 57. F minor.*
Allo. assai. (♩. — 126.)

24. *Op. 78. F♯ major.*
Ado. cantabile. (♪ — 76.)

25. *Op. 79. G major.*
Presto alla Tedesca. (♩. — 84.)

26. *Op. 81. E♭ major.*
Ado. (♪ — 72.) Das Lebewohl.

27. *Op. 90. E minor.*
Allegro. (♩ — 160.)

28. *Op. 101. A major.*
Alltto. ma non troppo.(♩. — 80.)

29. *Op. 106. B♭ major.*
Allegro. (♩ — 138.)

30. *Op. 109. E major.*
Vivace ma non troppo. (♩ — 112.)

31. *Op. 110. A♭ major.*
Modo. cantabile molto espress. (♩ — 63.)

32. *Op. 111. C minor.*
Maestoso. (♩ — 56.)

33. *No. 1. E♭ major.*
Allegro cantabile.

34. *No. 2. F minor.*
Larghetto maestoso.

35. *No. 3. D major.*
Allegro.

36. *C. major.*
Allegro.

37. *No. 1. G major.*
Sonatine. Moderato.

38. *No. 2. F. major.*
Sonatine. Allegro assai.

MENDELSSOHN'S SONGS WITHOUT WORDS.

1ᵉʳ Recueil.

Op. 19.

2ᵈ Recueil.

Op. 30.

7. Contemplation	Andante espressivo		E flat major.
8. Sans Repos	Allegro di molto		B flat minor.
9. Consolation	Andante sostenuto		E major.
10. L'Egarée	Agitato e con fuoco		B minor.
11. Le Ruisseau	Andante grazioso		D major.
12. 2ᵈ Barcarolle	Allegretto tranquillo		F sharp minor.

3ᵈ Recueil.

Op. 38.

13. L'Etoile du Soir	Con moto	E flat major.
14. Bonheur perdu	Allegro non troppo	C minor.
15. La Harpe du Poète	Presto e molto vivace	E major.
16. Espoir	Andante	A major.
17. Appassionato	Agitato	A minor.
18. Duetto	Andante con moto	A flat major.

4ᵗʰ Recueil.

Op. 53.

19. Sur la Plage	Andante con moto	A flat major.
20. Le Nuage	Allegro non troppo	E flat major.
21. Presto Agitato	Presto	G minor.
22. Tristesse de l'Ame	Adagio	F minor.
23. Chant Triomphal	Allegro con fuoco	A minor.
24. La Fuite	Molto Allegro vivace	A major.

5ᵗʰ Recueil.

Op. 62.

25. Brise de Mai	Andante espressivo	G major.
26. Le Départ	Allegro con fuoco	B flat major.
27. Marche Funèbre	Andante maestoso	E minor.
28. Chant du Matin	Allegro con anima	G major.
29. 3ᵈ Barcarolle	Andante con moto	A minor.
30. Chanson de Printemps	Allegretto grazioso	A major.

6ᵗʰ Recueil.

Op. 67.

31. Méditation	Andante	E flat major.
32. Illusions perdues	Allegro leggiero	F sharp minor.
33. Chant du Pélerin	Andante tranquillo	B flat major.
34. La Fileuse	Presto	C major.
35. La Plainte du Pâtre	Moderato	B minor.
36. Sérénade	Allegretto non troppo	E major.

7ᵗʰ Recueil.

Op. 85.

37. Rêverie	Andante espressivo	F major
38. Les Adieux	Allegro agitato	A minor.
39. Délire	Presto	E flat major.
40. Elégie	Andante sostenuto	D major.
41. Le Retour	Allegretto	A major.
42. Chant du Voyageur	Allegretto con moto	B flat major.

See " Names of the Most Eminent Musicians," pages 8 and 9. One may safely choose among the works of these composers.

MUSICAL DICTIONARY.

Note. — In terms composed of several words, one modifying another, find the definition of each word.

ABBREVIATIONS.

a 2. . . .	Accent the two notes over which is "a 2"
A 3. . . .	A tre.
Accel. . . .	Accellerando.
Ad. lib. . .	Ad libitum.
Ad°. . . .	Adagio.
Affet° . . .	Affettuoso.
Affret° . . .	Affrettando.
Alt.	Alta.
Allo. . . .	Allegro.
Alltto . . .	Allegretto.
All 8va. . .	All' ottava.
Al Seg. . .	Al Segno.
Andno . . .	Andantino.
Andte . . .	Andante.
Arp°. . .	Arpeggio.
A tem. . .	A tempo.
A temp. . .	A tempo.

A	[It.]	By. For. In. In a.
Abbandono .	[It.]	Despondingly.
Abwesenheit .	[G.]	Absence.
A Battuta .	[It.]	In strict time.
A Bene Placito	[It.]	At pleasure as to time.
A Capriccio .	[It.]	At will or fancy.
Accellerando .	[It.]	Increase the speed gradually.
Accent		A stress placed upon a note or passage.
Accentato . .	[It.]	Accented.
Accompaniment . .		A part added to a principal one to enhance the effect of the composition.
Adagio . .	[It.]	Slow.
Adagissimo .	[It.]	Very slow.
Ad Libitum .	[L.]	At will. It implies that the time of some particular passage is left to the taste of the performer; also that sometimes embellishments may be introduced.
Affetto . . .	[It.]	Affection.
Affettuosamente	[It.]	Affectionately.
Affettuoso .	[It.]	Affectionate.
Afflizione . .	[It.]	Sorrow. Affliction.
Affrettando .	[It.]	Hurrying the time.
Affrettate . .	[It.]	Hurry the time.
Agevole . .	[It.]	Light. Easy. Without labor.
Agitato . .	[It.]	Anxious. With agitation.
Agitazione . .	[It.]	Agitation. Anxiety.
Air		An air. A melody. A theme.
Ais	[G.]	"A" sharp.
Al } All' } . . . Alla }	[It.]	To the. In the style of.

All' ottava .	[It.]	To the octave.
Allegramente.	[It.]	Gayly. Lively.
Allegretto . .	[It.]	Cheerful and rather quick movement or tempo, but less so than allegro.
Allegrezza	[It.]	Joyfully. Cheerfully.
Allegrissimo .	[It.]	Very quick and lively.
Allegro . .	[It.]	Quick. Lively. It implies a rapid and vivacious movement, often modified by the addition of other words. (See "Note")
Al Segno, or } this sign ⌢ }		Signifies that the performer must repeat from a similar sign to the word "Fine," or to a pause thus ⌢ over a double bar.
Alta . . .	[It.]	High. Higher.
Alternativo .	[It.]	Alternately.
Alto		See Viola, page 12; also Contralto, page 13.
Alto Clef		C clef on the third line. (See page 28.)
Amabile . .	[It.]	Amiable.
Amarezza . .	[It.]	Bitterness.
Amore . . .	[It.]	Love.
Amorevole . .	[It.]	Gentle. Graceful.
Amorevolmente	[It.]	Amiably.
Amoroso . .	[It.]	Affectionate.
Amphibrach . . .		A musical foot, containing one short, one long, and one short note.
Amphimacer . . .		A musical foot, containing one long, one short, and one long note.
Anapest		A musical foot, containing two short notes followed by one long note.
Ancora . .	[It.]	Again.
Andante . .	[It.]	Neither fast nor slow. Indicates a gentle style; it is often modified by the addition of other words. (See "Note.")
Andantino .	[It.]	Somewhat faster than andante, but slower than allegretto.
Angosciamento	[It.]	Anxiety.
Anhang . .	[G.]	A sort of coda. (See Coda.)
Anima . . .	[It.]	Soul. Feeling.
Animato . .	[It.]	Spirited.
Animoso . .	[It.]	Energetic.
Anleitung . .	[G.]	Introduction.
Antico . . .	[It.]	Ancient.
Appassionato } Appassionata- } [It.] mente }		Intensity of feeling.
Appoggiata .	[It.]	Dwelt upon.
Appoggiature	[It.]	(See page 75.)
Arco . . .	[It.]	The bow. It implies to resume playing with the bow after a "pizzicato."
Ardito . . .	[It.]	Bold. Energetic.
Aria . . .	[It.]	An air. A melody.

Arietta . . .	[It.]	A short light air.
Arioso . . .	[It.]	Melodious.
Armonico }		
Armonioso } .	[It.]	Harmonious.
Armonious }		
Armoniosamente	[It.]	Harmoniously.
Arpa . . .	[It.]	Harp.
Arpeggiando }		
Arpeggiato }	[It.]	(See pages 24 and 52.)
Arpeggio }		
Articulatato .	[It.]	Articulated. Distinctly played.
As	[G.]	"A" flat. .
Asprezza . .	[It.]	Dryly. Severe. Stern.
Assai . . .	[It.]	Very. Extremely.
A tempo . .	[It.]	In time. This term is generally met after a "ritard," and indicates to resume the original degree of movement.
A tre . . .	[It.]	For three voices or instruments.
Attacca }	[It.]	It implies that after a short pause, what follows must be begun suddenly and with great firmness although a soft tone might be required.
Attacca Subito }		
Audace . .	[It.]	Bold.
Aus	[G.]	From. Out of.
Ausdruck .	[G.]	Expression.
A Vista . .	[It.]	At sight.

ABBREVIATION.

Brill. . . .		Brillante.

Badinage . .	[F.]	Playfulness.
Ballad		A short and familiar song. A lyric poem set to music. (See Lyric.)
Barcarolle .	[It.]	Airs sung by the Venetian gondoliers while following their avocations; generally in ⁶⁄₈ measure.
Bassi . . .	[It.]	Double Basses. (See page 12.) It also implies that the Double Basses are to resume playing.
Basso . . .	[It.]	Double-bass. (See page 12; also Bass part.)
Bassone }	[It.]	Bassoon or Fagotto. (See page 12.)
Bassoon }		
Battuta . .	[It.]	Time. The beat.
Begeisterung .	[G.]	Exaltation. Excitement.
Begleitung .	[G.]	Accompaniment.
Bellezza . .	[It.]	Beauty. Beautiful.
Ben. . . .	[It.]	Well. Particularly. Very.
Bizzaro . .	[It.]	Capricious. Fantastic.
Bolero . . .	[It.]	A ⁴⁄₄ measure Spanish dance with castanets; so called from the name of its originator.
Bow		The stick holding the hair, which, by passing over the strings of a violin or other instrument, produces the sound.
Bravura . .	[It.]	Bravely. Spirited.
Brillante . .	[It.]	Brilliantly. With eclat.
Brio }	[It.]	Spirited. With vigor.
Brioso }		
Buffa }	[It.]	Comic.
Buffo }		
Bugle		Hunting or Military Horn.
Burlando . .	[It.]	In a jesting manner.

ABBREVIATIONS.

Calan. }		Calando.
Cal⁰. } . .		
C. B. .		Contrabasso.
Celli . . .		Violoncelli. Violoncellos.
Cello . . .		Violoncello.
Clar. }		Clarinet.
Cl. }		
Col. C. . .		Col Canto.
Col. }		Colla.
Coll'. }		
Cres. . . .		Crescendo.
C⁰. . . .		Concerto.

Caccia .	[It.]	Hunting style.
Cadence }	[It.]	(See Cadences, page 57.) Also an ornamental passage in a song or piece, generally written in small notes; sometimes extemporaneous.
Cadenza }		
Calando . .	[It.]	Diminish both tone and movement gradually.
Calcando . .	[It.]	Hurry the time.
Calmato . .	[It.]	Calm. Tranquil.
Calore . . .	[It.]	Warm. Animated. With fire.
Caminando .	[It.]	Flowing.
Canon		(See page 14.)
Cantabile . .	[It.]	Graceful. Melodious.
Cantando . .	[It.]	In a singing style.
Cantata . .	[It.]	A vocal composition of several movements, comprising Recitatives, Airs, etc.
Canto . . .	[It.]	Voice. Part.
Canzone . .	[It.]	A song.
Canzonetta .	[It.]	A short and light song.
Capo . . .	[It.]	Beginning.
Capriccio . .	[It.]	A capricious, fanciful composition.
Capricciosa-mente }	[It.]	Capriciously.
Capriccioso .	[It.]	Capricious.
Capriccietto .	[It.]	A short capriccio.
Carattere . .	[It.]	Character.
Carillon . .	[F.]	Chimes of bells.
Carol		An antique song. A song of joy and exultation. A song of devotion. A hymn. A light song. A lay.
Castagnets }		Hollow shells used in Spain to accompany dance tunes or songs.
Castanets }		
Cavatina . .	[It.]	A short melody or air, occasionally preceded by a recitative.
Celerita . .	[It.]	Swiftness. Quickness.
Celli . . .	[It.]	(plu.) Violóncelli. It also implies that the Violoncellos are to play while the Double-basses are to be silent.
Cello . . .	[It.]	Violoncello.
Cembalo . .	[It.]	Harpsichord, having been improved was called cembalo, later clavecin, and finally piano.
Ces	[G.]	"C" flat.
Chant . . .	[F.]	Air. Song. Melody.
Chasse . . .	[F.]	Hunting.
Che . . .	[It.]	Than.
Chiudendo .	[It.]	Closing. Ending with.
Choral . . .		For many voices.
Chord		(See page 51.)
Cis	[G.]	"C" Sharp.
Civetteria . .	[It.]	Coquettishly.

Clarinet } Clarionet }	. .	(See page 12.)
Clavecin } Clavicembalo }	. .	(See Cembalo.)
Coda . . .	[It.]	A passage added after the end of a piece or movement.
Col Canto .	[It.]	Implies that the accompanist must follow the singer in regard to time.
Colla . . .	[It.]	With.
Colla parte } Colla voce }	[It.]	Implies that the accompanist must follow the principal part or voice in regard to time.
Come	[It.]	As.
Commodo } Commoda- } mente }	. [It.]	Quietly.
Common Time . . .		4 beats and 4 quarter notes in a bar; expressed by the figures ⁴⁄₄.
Compiacevole	[It.]	Pleasing. Agreeable.
Con	[It.]	With.
Concert . . .		A musical entertainment in which a number of musicians take part.
Concerto . .	[It.]	(See page 15.)
Consolante .	[It]	Comforting. Encouraging.
Consonance .		An interval agreeable to the ear.
Contra-Basso	[It.]	Double-Bass. (See page 12.)
Contratänze .	[G.]	Contredanses. Quadrilles.
Contralto		The lowest of female and the highest of male voices; also called counter-tenor.
Contrapunckt	[G.]	} Counterpoint. (See pages 7 and 14.)
Contrapunto .	[It.]	
Contrepoint .	[F.]	
Contredanse .	[F.]	Quadrille. Cotillon.
Cor	[F.]	Horn. (See page 12.)
Corda . . .	[It.]	} String.
Corde . . .	[F.]	
Cor de chasse	. .	French horn.
Corna Musa .	[It.]	Bagpipe.
Cornet } Cornett }	. [It.]	Horn. A sort of trumpet.
Cornet a piston	[F.]	Trumpet with valves.
Corni } Corno }	. [It.]	Horn. (See page 12.)
Corona . .	[It.]	A pause.
Corte . . .	[It.]	Short. Quickly played.
Coulé . . .	[F.]	Very legato. (See page 19.)
Counterpoint . .		(See pages 7 and 14.)
Counter Tenor . .		The highest of male and the lowest
Counter tenor } Clef }	. .	of female voices. C clef on the third line.
Cremona . .	[It.]	A small town in Italy celebrated as having been the residence of the great violin-makers: Amati, Straduarius, Guarnerius, etc.
Crescendo .	[It.]	Increase the tone gradually. (See page 61.)
Crooks		Small curved tubes, applied to horns, trumpets, etc., to change their pitch.

ABBREVIATIONS.

D. C. . . .	Da Capo.
Decres. . .	Decrescendo.
Delicatiss. .	Delicatissimo.
Diap. . . .	Diapason.

Dim. . . .	Diminuendo.
Dol.	Dolce.
Dolciss. . .	Dolcissimo.
D. S. . . .	Dal Segno.

Da.	[It.]	By. From the.
Da Capo . .	[It.]	From the beginning. It indicates to repeat and finish with the first strain.
Dactyl		A musical foot containing one long and two short notes.
Dal	[It.]	By. From. From the.
Dal Segno .	[It.]	Indicates to repeat from the sign.
Das	[G.]	The.
Deciso . . .	[It.]	Decided. Determined.
Decrescendo .	[It.]	Decrease the tone gradually. (See page 61.)
Delicatemente	[It.]	Delicately.
Delicatezza .	[It.]	Delicacy.
Delicatissimo .	[It.]	With extreme delicacy.
Delicato . .	[It.]	Delicate.
Des	[G.]	" D " flat.
Deutsche . .	[G.]	German.
Destra . . .	[It.]	} Right. The right hand.
Dextra . . .	[L.]	
Devoto . . .	[It.]	Devout.
Devozione . .	[It.]	Devotion.
Di	[It.]	Of.
Diapason . . .		Compass of a voice or of an instrument. The different pitch between voices or instruments. Name of certain stops of an organ. Name of a tuning-fork in French.
Di Grado . .	[It.]	By Degrees. Gradually.
Diluendo . .	[It.]	Diminish the tone gradually until it is inaudible.
Diminuendo .	[It.]	Diminish the tone gradually.
Di molto . .	[It.]	Very, as: Allegro di molto, very quick.
Dis	[G.]	" D " sharp.
Discord . . .		A dissonant combination of sounds.
Disperato . .	[It.]	Despairingly.
Disperazione .	[It.]	Despair.
Dissonance . . .		A discord.
Divertissement	[F.]	A light recreating composition.
Divisi . . .	[It]	When a passage in an orchestral composition is written in octaves or other intervals it implies that half of the performers must play the upper notes, while the other half play the lower ones.
Divotamente .	[It]	Piously.
Divoto . . .	[It.]	Pious.
Divozione . .	[It.]	Devotion.
Dolce . . .	[It]	Soft. Gentle. Sweet tone.
Dolce Dolce .	[It.]	Little by little.
Dolcemente .	[It.]	Softly. Sweetly.
Dolcezza . .	[It.]	Sweetness.
Dolcissimo .	[It.]	With extreme sweetness. Extremely soft.
Dolente . .	[It.]	Complaining. Unfortunate.
Dolore . . .	[It.]	Sorrow. Grief. Sadness.
Doloroso . .	[It.]	Sorrowful.
Dominant . . .		(See page 50.)
Doppia } Doppio }	[It.]	Double, as: Doppio movimento, twice as fast.
Double-bass .	. .	(See page 12.)
Dritto . . .	[It.]	Right. The right hand.

Due . . .	[It.]	Two.
Due Volta .	[It.]	Twice. Repeat.
Duet		A composition for two voices or instruments.
Duettino } Duetto }	[It.]	A short duet.
Duo. . . .	[It.]	A duet.
Duolo . . .	[It.]	Mourning. Sadness.
Dur	[G.]	Major.
Durate . . .	[It.]	Harsh.
Duramente .	[It.]	Harshly.
Durchgehend .	[G.]	Transient.
Duro . . .	[It.]	Disagreeable. Rude. Hard.

ABBREVIATIONS.

F. f. . . .	Forte, loud.
Ff. ff. . . .	Fortissimo, very loud.
Fff. fff. . . .	Very fortissimo, extremely loud.
Fag. . . .	Fagotto.
Fl. . . .	Flute.
Flau. . . .	Flauto.
For. . . .	Forte.
Forz. . . .	Forzando.
F. p. . . .	Forte, and then Piano (soft); when applied to a single note it indicates a strong accent.
Fz	Forzando.

ABBREVIATIONS.

Energ¹ . .	Energicamente.
Esp. . . .	Espressione.
Espress. . .	Espressivo.

E, Ed . . .	[It.]	And.
Ecossaise . .	[F.]	A Scotch air or dance.
Egualmente .	[It.]	Evenly. Equally.
Einfach . .	[G.]	Simple.
Eis . .	[G.]	"E" sharp.
Elegante . .	[It.]	Elegant.
Elegantemente	[It.]	Elegantly.
Eleganza . .	[It.]	Elegance.
Elegy		A poetical composition of mournful character. A mournful or funeral song.
Empfindung .	[G.]	Emotion.
Energia . .	[It.]	Energy.
Energicamente	[It.]	Energetically.
Energico . .	[It.]	Energetic.
Enge . . .	[G.]	Close. Condensed.
Epic.		A narrative poem, describing generally the exploits of heroes, as the Iliad and Odyssey of Homer. Sometimes spoken as a musical declamation.
Episode		A part of a composition not founded on the principal subject.
Epoi . . .	[It.]	And. Then.
Erhöhung . .	[G.]	Raising the pitch of a note by a sharp.
Erniedrigung	[G.]	Lowering the pitch of a note by a flat.
Erweitert . .	[G.]	Expanded. Extended.
Es	[G.]	"E" flat.
Eses . . .	[G.]	"E" double flat.
Espagnuolo .	[It.]	In the Spanish style.
Espressione .	[It.]	Expression.
Espressivo .	[It.]	Expressive.
Estinte } Estinto }	[It.]	Diminish gradually both tone and movement until the music becomes inaudible.
Estravaganza	[It.]	Extravagant. Wild.
Estremamente	[It.]	Extremely.
Et	[It.]	And.
Etwaslangsa- mer . . }	[G.]	A little slower.
Eufonia } Euphony }	[It.]	Sweetness. Harmonious.
Extempore .	[It.]	Extemporaneous.

Facilita . .	[It.]	An easier way to play a certain passage.
Fagotto . .	[It.]	Bassoon. (See page 12.)
Fandango . . .		Spanish dance in ⅜ measure, generally accompanied with castanets.
Fanfare		A trumpet's call. A flourish of trumpet.
Fantaisie . .	[F.] }	A species of composition in which the author gives free scope to his ideas without regard to those systematic and metrical forms which regulate other compositions.
Fantasia . .	[It.] }	
Fastosamente	[It.]	Proudly. In a grand style.
Fastoso . .	[It.]	Proud. Haughty.
Ferma . .	[It.]	Firm. Resolute.
Fermamente .	[It.]	Firmly.
Fermata . .	[It.]	A pause.
Feroce . .	[It.]	Fierce. Brave.
Ferocita . .	[It.]	Ferocity.
Fes . . .	[G.]	"F" flat.
Fieramente .	[It.]	Boldly. Proudly. Very energetic.
Fiero . . .	[It.]	Proud. Bold. Haughty.
Figured-bass .	.	(See page 14.)
Fin	[F.]	End. Conclusion.
Finale . . .	[It.]	Last movement of a musical work.
Fine . . .	[It.]	End. Conclusion.
Finito . . .	[It.]	Concluded. Ended.
Fis . . .	[G.]	"F" sharp.
Fisfis . . .	[G.]	"F" double sharp.
Flauto . . .	[It.]	Flute. (See page 12.)
Flebile . .	[It.]	Plaintive.
Flessibilita .	[It.]	Flexibility.
Florid		Ornament. Ornamental.
Flute		(See page 12.)
Focoso . .	[It]	With fire. Animated.
Forte . . .	[It.]	Loud.
Fortissimo .	[It.]	Very loud.
Forza . .	[It.]	Force. Power.
Forzando . .	[It.]	With force and emphasis.
Fresco . .	[It.]	Fresh. Young. Lively.
Fröhlicher .	[G]	Merry. Joyous.
Fuga	[It.]	Fugue. (See page 14.)
Fugato . . .	[It.]	In the fugue or severe style.
Fughetta . .	[It.]	A short fugue.
Fugue		(See page 14.)
Fundamental- bass }	. .	A bass formed of the roots of chords only.
Fuoco . . .	[It.]	Fire. Anger. Vehemence.
Furia . . .	[It.]	Furor.
Furioso . .	[It.]	Furious. Enraged.
Furlano . .	[It.]	An antiquated dance.
Furore . . .	[It.]	Furor.

ABBREVIATIONS.

Grand°	. .	Grandioso.
Graz°	. .	Grazioso.

Guracha	. .	[It.]	A species of dance.
Gusto	. . .	[It.]	Taste. Pleasing.
Gustosamente	.	[It.]	Agreeably.
Gustoso	. .	[It.]	Agreeable.

Gaiement	. .	[F.]	Cheerfully.
Gaio	. . .	[It.]	Gay. Cheerful.
Garbo	. . .	[It.]	With simplicity. Amiably.
Gavot *Gavotta* }	. .	[It.]	A lively dance in Common Time.
Genera	. .	[L.]	Plural of Genus.
Generoso	. .	[It.]	Generous.
Genus	. . .	[L.]	Class. Order. The different modes of dividing the octave, as by tones and semitones, Diatonic or natural genus; by semitones only, Chromatic or artificial genus; and theoretically by quarter tones only, Enharmonic genus. (See " Genera," page 49.)
Ges	. . . .	[G.]	" G " flat.
Geschwind	.	[G.]	Quick.
Giga *Gigue* }	. .	[It.]	A jig. A lively species of dance.
Giocosamente		[It.]	Sprightly. Humorously.
Giocoso	. .	[It.]	Gay. With sportiveness.
Giojoso	. .	[It.]	Joyous.
Giovale	. .	[It.]	Jovial.
Gis	. . . .	[G.]	" G " sharp.
Giusto	. . .	[It.]	Even and in strict time. Well balanced.
Glee	. . . . .		A cheerful composition for several voices.
Glissando	. .	[It.]	Gliding.
Glissicato	. .	[It.]	Gentle and gliding.
Gondellied	.	[G.]	A Barcarolle. (See Barcarolle.)
Gondoliere	.	[It.]	Venetian Boatman.
Gondoline	. . . .		A Barcarolle. (See Barcarolle.)
Gong	. . . . .		An Indian pulsatile instrument, consisting of a large circular plate of bell metal.
Graces	. . . . .		Embellishments or ornaments. (See Melodic Ornaments, page 75.)
Grandioso	.	[It.]	Grand. Splendid.
Gran Gusto	.	[It.]	In a grand and noble style.
Gravamente	.	[It.]	Gravely. With dignity.
Grave	. . .	[It.]	Solemn. Grave. An extremely slow and solemn movement or tempo. The slowest degree of movement. (See Larghissimo.)
Gravita	. .	[It.]	Dignity. Gravity.
Grazia	. . .	[It.]	Grace. Elegance.
Graziosamente		[It.]	Gracefully.
Graziosetto	.	[It.]	In a graceful style.
Grazioso	. .	[It.]	Graceful. Amiable.
Gregorian Chant or *Plain Chant.* }		(See page 5.)
Grosse	. . .	[G.]	Grand.
Grosso	. . .	[It.]	Great. Grand.
Ground	. . . .		A bass, consisting of a few simple notes, intended as a theme on which, at each repetition, a new melody is constructed.
Group *Gruppetto* *Gruppo* }	.	[It.]	Group. (See page 76.)
Guitar	. . . .		An instrument somewhat like a violin. It has six strings, and is played upon with the fingers.

H	. . . .		This letter is used by the Germans for " B " natural.
Harmonium	. .	.	A Melodeon. (See Melodeon.)
Harmony	. . . .		(See pages 13 and 14.)
Harp	. . . . .		A large stringed instrument of a triangular shape. Played with the fingers.
His	. . . .	[G.]	" B " sharp.
Homophony	. .		In unison.
Hopswalzer	.	[G.]	Quick waltzes.
Horn	. . . . .		(See page 12.)
Hyper	. . .	[Gr.]	Above. Over.
Hypo	. . .	[Gr.]	Below. Under.

ABBREVIATION.

Introd	. . .	Introduzione.

I	. . . .	[It.]	With. In the.
Idylle	. . . . .		A short descriptive composition on pastoral subjects.
Il	. . . . .	[It.]	The.
Imitation	. .	[F.] [It.]	} An imitation. (See page 14.)
Imitazione	.	
Impeto	. . .	[It.]	Impetuosity.
Impetuosamente	[It.]	Impetuously.
Impetuosita	.	[It.]	Impetuosity.
Impetuoso	. .	[It.]	Impetuous.
Imponente	. .	[It.]	Haughtily. Imposingly.
Impromptu	.	[F.] [It.]	} An extemporaneous composition.
Improvvisata	.	
In	. . . .	[It.]	In.
Inglese	. . .	[It.]	In the English style.
Innocente	. .	[It.]	Innocent. Artless.
Innocentemente	[It.]	Innocently. Simply.
Inquietamente	.	[It.]	Impatiently. Uneasily.
Inquiettezza	.	[It.]	Disquietude. Uneasiness.
Inquieto	.	[It.]	Uneasy. Perturbed.
Intensity	. . .		(See " Sound " in *Musical Dictionary.*)
Interlude	. . . .		) Intermediate. Between. A strain
Interludium	. .	[L.]	} introduced and performed between
Intermezzo	. .	[It.]	) others.
Interruzione	.	[It.]	Interruption.
Interval	. . .		(See page 37.)
Intonation	. . .		(See " Sound " in *Musical Dictionary.*)
Intrada	. .	[It.]	)
Introduction	. .	[F.]	} An introductory strain or movement.
Introduzione	.	[It.]	)
Introducimento	[It.]	Introduction.
Inversion	. . .		(See page 54.)
Irare	. . . .	[It.]	Angry.
Iratamente	.	[It.]	Angrily.
Irresoluto	. .	[It.]	Undecided. Irresolutely.
Istesso	. . .	[It.]	The same.

Jaeger-chor .	[G.]	Hunting chorus.
Jew's Harp . . .		A small instrument made of brass or steel, and shaped as a lyre; when played, it is placed between the teeth and struck with the fore-finger.
Jig		A quick movement in compound measure of $\frac{6}{8}$ or $\frac{1}{2}\frac{2}{8}$. (See Compound Measure, page 47.)
Jingles		Loose pieces of tin placed around a tamborine to increase the sound.
Jubilee		A time of rejoicing.

Kapellmeister	[G.]	Chapel master.
Key		(See pages 49, 63, and 64.)
Key		The lever by which the notes of a key-board are made to sound. Flutes, Oboes, and other wind instruments have also their keys, by which certain holes are opened or shut.
Key-board . . .		(See page 27.)
Key-note		(See page 50.)

ABBREVIATIONS.

Leg. . . .	Legato.
Legg. . . .	Leggerezza.
Leggier. . .	Leggiero.
L. H. . . .	Left hand.

La	[It.]	The.
Lagrimoso .	[It.]	Sorrowful.
Lamentabile .	[It.]	Plaintively.
Lamentazione .	[It.]	Lamentation.
Lamentevole .	[It.]	Complaining.
Lamentoso .	[It.]	Sad. Sorrowful.
Landler . .	[G.]	A country dance or air, generally in $\frac{3}{4}$ measure.
Landmann . .	[G.]	Farmer.
Langueggiare	[It.]	Becoming languid.
Languidamente	[It.]	Languishingly.
Languido . .	[It.]	Languid.
Largamente .	[It.]	Nobly. Generously. In a full broad style.
Larghetto . .	[It.]	Slow. A slow and measured movement or tempo; but less so than largo.
Larghissimo .	[It.]	Extremely slow. An extremely slow movement or tempo. The slowest degree of movement. (See Grave.)
Largo . . .	[It.]	Very slow. A very slow movement or tempo. Grand. Noble.
Lay		A song. A joyous lay.
Le	[It.]	The.
Leading note . . .		(See page 50.)
Lebewohl . .	[G.]	Farewell.
Lebhaft . .	[G.]	Lively.
Legatissimo .	[It.]	Very legato. (See page 19.)
Legato . . .	[It.]	(See page 19.)
Leggerezza .	[It.]	Lightness.
Leggiadro . .	[It.]	Graceful.
Leggierissimo	[It.]	Extremely light and easy (very clear.)
Leggiermente	[It.]	Lightly.
Leggiero . .	[It.]	Light.
Leicht . . .	[G.]	Easy.

Lentamente .	[It.]	Slowly.
Lentando . .	[It.]	With increased slowness.
Lento . . .	[It.]	Slow. Very slow.
Lentezza . .	[It.]	Slowness. In a sedate and lingering pace.
Lied . . .	[G.]	Song.
L'istesso tempo	[It.]	In the same tempo as previously.
Loco		(See page 24.)
Lugubre . .	[It.]	Mournful.
Lunga pausa	[It.]	A long pause.
Lungo . .	[It.]	Long. Continuous.
Lusingando .	[It.]	Persuasively. Soothingly.
Lyric		A poem composed for musical recitation, particularly that in which the composer expresses his own thoughts and feelings. Sung to the lyre by the ancients.

ABBREVIATIONS.

Maest^o . . .	Maestoso.
Magg. . . .	Maggiore.
Man^{do} . . .	Mancando.
Marcatiss. .	Marcatissimo.
M. D. . . .	Mano Dritta, Right hand.
M. F. . ' . .	Mezzo Forte, Rather loud.
M. G. . . .	Left hand.
M. M. . . .	Maelzel's Metronome. (See page 15.)
M. P. . . .	Mezzo piano, Rather soft.
M. S. . . .	Mano sinistra, Left hand.
Men. . . .	Meno.
Min. . . .	Minore.
Mod^o . . .	Moderato.
M. V., or *m. v.*	Mezza voce, Moderately loud.

Ma . .	[It.]	But.
Madrigale .	[It.]	Elaborate composition for voices in five or six parts, in the ancient style of imitation and fugue.
Madrigals . . .		
Maestoso . .	[It.]	With majesty. A slow and solemn movement or tempo.
Maggiore .	[It.]	Major. (See "Table of Intervals" page 53.)
Majeur . .	[F.]	
Major . .		
Major mode . . .		One of the two modern modes; that in which the third from the key-note is major. (See pages 65 and 68.)
Malincolico .	[It.]	Melancholic.
Malinconia .	[It.]	Melancholy.
Mancando .	[It.]	Decrease the tone gradually.
Mandolino .	[It.]	Very similar to a guitar, has four strings. Played with the fingers.
Mano . . .	[It.]	The hand.
Manual . .	[G.]	Key-board.
Marcatissimo	[It.]	Very much accented. Strongly marked.
Marcato . .	[It.]	Marked. Accented.
Marche . .	[F.]	A march. In harmony, a symmetrical sequence of chords is called "Marche."
March . . .		A march. A military air played to regulate the steps and to animate the soldiers.
Marche . .	[It.]	
Marcia . .	[It.]	
Marsch . .	[G.]	
Martel'ato .	[It.]	Over accented. Hammered like.
Marziale . .	[It.]	In a martial style.

Mazourk . .	[P.]	A quick Polish dance in ⅜ measure,
Mazurka . .	.G.	with a peculiar rhythmic construc-
Mazureck. . . .		tion, somewhat like that of a po-
		lacca.
Medessimo .	[It.]	The same.
Mediant		(See page 50.)
Melodeon		A portable organ very similar in shape to a square piano, but smaller. Having one or more key-boards. Also called Harmonium, Seraphine, etc.
Melody		An air. A theme.
Meno . . .	[It.]	Less; Meno mosso : slower.
Menuet . .	[F.]	(See Minuet.)
Messa di voce.	[It.]	A swelling and diminishing of the voice on a long holding note.
Mesto . . .	[It.]	Sadness. Grief.
Mestoso . .	[It.]	Sad. Mournful.
Metronome . . .		(See Metronome of Maelzel, page 15.)
Mezza voce .	[It.]	Moderately loud.
Mezzo . . .	[It.]	Middling. Rather. Half.
Mezzo soprano	[It.]	A female voice lower in pitch than the soprano but higher than the contralto.
Minaccioso .	[It.]	Threatening.
Mineur . .	[F.]	Minor. (See " Alteration of the major intervals," page 54.)
Minor		
Minore . .	[It.]	
Minor Mode . .		One of the two modern modes ; that in which the third from the key-note is minor. (See pages 65 and 68.)
Minuet.		A slow, stately, but graceful dance.
Minuetto . .	[It.]	Also one of the movements of certain musical compositions, in ¾ measure.
Misterioso .	[It.]	Mysterious.
Misurato . .	[It.]	Strict time.
Mit	[G.]	With.
Mode		(See page 65)
Moderato . .	[It.]	Not too fast. Moderate.
Modestamente	[It.]	Modestly. Quietly.
Modesto . .	[It.]	Modest. Simple.
Modulation . . .		A change of key.
Moll . . .	[G.]	Minor.
Molto . . .	[It.]	Very. Extremely. Very much.
Monochord . . .		An instrument with only one string.
Monocordo .	[It.]	On only one string.
Mordant . . .		(See page 75.)
Mordente . .	[It.]	
Morendo . .	[It.]	Dying away. Decrease gradually both tone and movement until it dies away.
Morisco . .	[It.]	In the Moorish style.
Mormoramento	[It.]	Murmur.
Mormorando	[It.]	Gently murmuring. Murmuringly.
Mosso . . .	[It.]	Movement. Speed.
Moto . . .	[It.]	Agitation. Activity. Movement.
Moto contrario	[It.]	Contrary motion. One part ascends while another descends.
Motteggiando	[It.]	Jeeringly. Playfully.
Motteggio . .	[It.]	Playfulness. Sportiveness.
Movement. . .		Tempo, or degree of speed. Also name given to the different parts of a musical work. (See Symphony, page 15.)
Movimento .	[It.]	
Musette . .	[F.]	A small kind of bag-pipe. Also an air of sweet and pastoral character.
Naccare . . .	[It.]	Castanets.
Negghittosamente	[It.]	Carelessly.

Negghittoso .	[It.]	Careless.
Negglettamente	[It.]	Negligently.
Negligente .	[It.]	Negligent.
Nel		
Nella		[It.] In the.
Nelle		
Nettamente .	[It.]	Clearly. Particularly clear and distinct.
Nobile . . .	[It.]	Noble.
Nobilmente .	[It.]	Nobly.
Nocturne . .	[F.]	A vocal or instrumental composition of an elegant, light and fanciful character, suitable for an evening recreation.
Nocturno . .	[It.]	
Non . . .	[It.]	No. Not.
Nonetto . .	[It.]	A composition in nine parts.
Notation		The art of representing musical sounds and their various modifications by notes, rests, signs, etc.
Notes		(See page 27.)

Ob.		Oboe.
Op.		Opus.
Orgº		Organo.
8, 8ª, 8ʳª . .		Octava. Ottava. (See page 24.)
O	[It.]	Or.
Obligato . .	[It.]	Of Obligation. Must play. Must be played.
Oboe		(See page 12.)
Octava		Ottava. Octave. To the octave. (See page 24.)
Octave		The interval comprised between a given note and the same note repeated eight notes above, as : between two C's or two D's, etc. (See page 27.)
Ode	[Gr.]	A short song or poem. A lyric composition.
Œuvre		(See Opus.)
Ohne . . .	[G.]	Without.
Ondeggiamento	[It.]	Waving the sound. Tremulous sound.
Opera		See Opus.
Opera (Grand) . .		A musical drama consisting of an overture, recitatives, airs, choruses, etc., combined with scenery, acting, etc.
Opera (Comic) . .		A musical comedy consisting of an overture, airs, choruses, etc., combined with scenery and acting, but in which there are no recitatives, that part of the opera being spoken.
Ophicleide . . .		A brass instrument of a loud tone and a deep pitch ; chiefly used in military music.
Opus . . .	[L.]	This word is applied to any composition of an author, as : Opus 1, opera 1, Œuvre 1, Op. 1, first work ; Opus 2, second work.
Oratorio . .	[It.]	A musical drama founded on some Scriptural subject, performed without scenery or action.
Orchestra		(See pages 11 and 12.)
Ordinario . .	[It.]	Usual.

Organ	}	Organ. The noblest of all musi-
Organo. . .	[It.]	cal instruments, chiefly used in
Orgel . . .	[G.]	churches. The organ is a large
Orgue . . .	[F.]	wind-instrument blown by bellows, having one, two or more keyboards, with rows of stops on either side, which when open allow the air to enter into the different pipes.
Ornaments . . .		Embellishments. (See Melodic Ornaments, page 75.)
O sia . . .	[It.]	Or else. It indicates a different manner of playing a passage; most generally an easier manner.
Osservanza .	[It.]	Very exact in regard to time.
Ottava . . .	[It.]	Octave. To the octave. (See page 24.)
Ouverture . .	[F.]	} An overture is the introduction to an opera, oratorio, etc.; written in the symphony style, and gives a general idea of the work which it introduces.
Overtura . .	[It.]	
Overture		

ABBREVIATIONS.

P.		Piano, soft.
PP. . . .		Pianissimo, very soft.
PPP. . . .		Very Pianissimo, extremely soft.
Ped. . . .		Pedal.
Perden. . .		Perdendosi.
PF. . . .		Piano and then Forte.
Pizz. . . .		Pizzicato.
1ma		Prima.
1mo		Primo.
Prestmo . . .		Prestissimo.

Parlando } Parlante }	. [It.]	In a speaking or declamatory manner.
Parte . .	[It.]	A part in vocal or instrumental music.
Partition .	[F.]	
Partitur .	[G.]	} Partition or Score. (See page 15.)
Partitura . .	[It.]	
Partizione . .	[It.]	
Passionate . .	[It.]	With pathos.
Passione . .	[It.]	Pathos.
Patetico . .	[It.]	} Pathetic.
Pathétique . .	[F.]	
Pastorale . .	[It.]	A rural movement.
Pause		(See page 61)
Pavane		A serious and antiquated French dance.
Pedal		(See page 14.)
Pedal		(See " Ped." page 25.) When one of the keys of a piano is pressed down, the hammer connected with it by a lever, strikes the strings of that key, thus producing a sound which ceases by a damper being lowered on the strings as soon as the key rises. By press ing down the pedal all the dampers are kept from the strings, consequently the sound of each note is more powerful and lasting. but becomes confused when the pedal is kept down too long at a time or pressed down too often.

		When breathing, (See " General Rules for the Oratorical Accent," page 60,) when the harmony changes, etc., the foot must leave the pedal. (See " Piano," also " Una Corda " in Musical Dictionary)
Pedali . .	[It.]	Pedals. Use both pedals.
Per	[It.]	For. By.
Perdendo } Perdendosi }	. [It.]	Diminish gradually both tone and movement until it dies away.
Pesante . .	[It.]	Heavy. With importance and weight.
Phrase		See page 56.
Piacére . .	[It.]	At will. Indicates that the passage is to be played according to the performer's taste.
Piacévole . .	[It.]	Pleasing. Agreeable.
Piacimento .	[It.]	(See Piacére, also Ad Libitum.)
Piangendo .	[It.]	Plaintively.
Piangevole .	[It.]	Sad.
Piangevolmente	[It.]	Sadly.
Pianissimo .	[It.]	Very soft.
Piano . . .	[It.]	Soft.
* Piano		A stringed instrument resembling a harp placed inside of a case, having a key-board extending seven octaves and a quarter. Every key of a grand piano has three strings, with the exception of the lowest ones, some of which have but two and the very lowest ones but one string. (See " Pedal, " also " Una Corda " in Musical Dictionary.)
Piccino . .	[It.]	Small.
Picciolo . .	[It.]	Small. Little.
Piccolo . .	[It.]	Small. Short.
Piéno . .	[It.]	Full.
Pietosaménte	[It.]	Compassionately.
Pietoso . .	[It.]	Compassionate.
Pitch		(See page 10.)
Piu	[It.]	More; Piu mosso, faster. Piu tosto lento, rather slower.
Pizzicato . .	[It.]	It indicates to twitch the string with the fingers, instead of playing with the bow.
Placidamente .	[It.]	Tranquilly.
Placidezza .	[It.]	Tranquillity. Sweetness.
Placidita .	[It.]	Quietude. Sweetness.
Placido . .	[It.]	Quiet. Sweet.
Plain Chant . .		Gregorian Chant. (See page 5)
Plaintivo . .	[It.]	Plaintive. Somewhat sad and complaining.
Pochettino } Pochetto }	. [It.]	A little.
Poco . .	[It.]	Little. A little. Somewhat. Rather.
Poco a poco. .	[It.]	By degrees. Little by little. Gradually.
Poggiato . .	[It.]	Dwelt upon. Impressive.
Poi	[It.]	Then. After. Afterwards.
Point d'orgue	[F.]	Pause. (See page 61.) A pedal passage ; that is, a note held in the bass while others are being played.
Polacca . .	[It.]	} A slow Polish dance in ¾ measure, of peculiar rhythmical construction, usually terminating on the third quarter note of the measure.
Polonaise . .	[F.]	
Pomposo . .	[It.]	In a grand and pompous style.
Portamento .	[It.]	It indicates to sustain and carry the sound to the next one.
Portante . .	[It.]	Sustaining.

* Dampness, drafts, and intense heat, will put the best tuned piano out of order. Always close the piano when through playing. Good care will save much tuning, but a piano should be tuned as soon as it needs it. See " Noise when playing," page 11.

Posato . . . [It.] Steady and gentle.

Post-horn . . [G.] A sort of bugle; also a movement suited to and imitating the notes of such an instrument.

Potpourri . . . . A medley. A piece where several parts of a work, mostly the favorite airs, are brought in.

Precipitato . [It.] Hurried. Accelerated.

Precisione. . [It.] Precision. Exactitude.

Prelude . . . . An introductory movement.

Prestezza . . [It.] Rapidity. Quickness.

Prestissimo . [It.] Extremely fast. An extremely quick movement or tempo. The most rapid degree of movement.

Presto . . . [It.] Very fast. A very quick movement or tempo.

Prima } . . [It.] First.
Primo }

Pronunziato . [It.] Accented. Well marked or articulated.

Puntamente . [It.] Very exact.

Puntato . . [It.] Detached. Particularly clear.

Quadrille . . [F.] Cotillon.

Quartet . . . . } A composition for four voices or instruments.
Quartette . . . }
Quartetto . . [It.] }

Quasi . . . [It.] In the manner or style of. Almost like.

Quasimente . [It.] Almost. Nearly like.

Quatuor . . [L.] See Quartette.

Questo . . . [It.] This. That.

Quieto . . . [It.] Calm. Quiet. With peace.

Quintet . . . . } A composition for five voices or instruments.
Quintetto . . [It.] }
Quintuor . . [F.] }

ABBREVIATIONS.

R. . . . . Right hand.

Raddol . . . Raddolcendo.

Rallen. } . . Rallentando.
Rallo }

Recit. . . . Recitativo.

R. H. . . . Right hand.

Rf. } . . Rinforzando.
Rfz. }
Rinf. }

Ritard . . . Ritardando.

Riten . . . Ritenuto.

Rabbia . . . [It.] Rage. Anger.

Raddolcendo } [It.] With increased softness.
Raddolcente }

Raddolcire . [It.] Softer and softer.

Rallentando . [It.] Gradually diminishing both tone and movement.

Rapidamente . [It.] Rapidly.

Rapidezza } [It.] Rapidity. Swiftness.
Rapidita }

Rapido. . . [It.] Rapid. Impetuous.

Rattamente . [It.] Promptly.

Rattemperare. [It.] Diminishing. Lessening. Moderating.

Rattenere . . [It.] Holding back. Restraining.

Ravvivando . [It.] Reviving. Reanimating and accelerating.

Recheat . . [It.] Name given to those sounds played

on the horn to recall the hounds from a false scent.

Recht . . . [G.] Right.

Recitando } . [It.] In the style of a recitative.
Recitante }

Recitatif . . [F.] } Recitative. That part of an opera,
Recitative . . . . } generally preceding an air, and a
Recitativo. . [It.] } kind of introduction to it, that is spoken on some notes. A musical declamation.

Reed . . . . . (See page 12.)

Reel. . . . . . A lively Scotch dance.

Register . . . . The compass of a voice or of an instrument. The different parts of that compass, as: the chest register, the middle register, and the head register. Also any of the stops of an organ.

Règle d'octave . . (See page 87.)

Relative Keys . . (See page 72.)

Religiosamente [It.] Religiously. Piously.

Religioso . . [It.] Pious. With religious feeling.

Repetizione . [It.] }
Replica . . [It.] } Repetition.
Reprise . . . [F.] }

Requiem . . [L.] A service for the dead; such as: Mozart's Requiem.

Resolution . . . . Is the concord which necessarily follows a discord. (See page 74)

Rest . . . . . (See page 33.)

Reverie . . . . . A musical musing. Wandering musical thoughts.

Rhapsodie . . . . A composition very similar to a potpourri, but of a somewhat higher order.

Rhythm . . . . . (See pages 13 and 56.)

Ricordanza . [It.] Remembrance. With recollection.

Rigore . . . [It.] Very severe and exact.

Rinforzando } [It.] With additional force and emphasis.
Rinforzato }

Risolutamente [It.] Resolutely. Decidedly.

Risolutezza . [It.] Resolution. Decision.

Risvegliato . [It.] With renewed animation.

Ritard . . . . Diminish the movement gradually. (See page 61.)

Ritardando } [It.] Diminish both tone and movement
Ritardato } gradually.

Ritenente } [It.] Ritard the movement, but not grad-
Ritenuto } ually.

Ritornello . . [It.] } A short introduction to a song or
Ritournelle . [F.] } to a dancing tune; the same being repeated between the verses, as well as at the end.

Romance . . [F.] } A short lyric tale set to music; or a
Romanza . . [It.] } simple and elegant melody suitable to such words.

Rondo . . . [It.] } A rondo generally consists of three
Rondeau . . [F.] } strains, the first being introduced at the end of each. It ends with the first strain in its original key.

Rondino . . [It.] A short and easy rondo.

Root. . . . . The "Fundamental" of a chord. (See page 51.)

Round . . . . . A sort of canon in unison.

Rubato } . . [It.] Borrowed. The term Tempo rubato
Robato } is applied to a style of performance in which some notes are held longer than their exact value, while that of others is curtailed, in order that the aggregate value of the measure may not be disturbed.

ABBREVIATIONS.

Scherz. . .	Scherzando.
Seg. . . .	Segno.
Sem. . . .	Sempre.
Sf . . .	Sforzando.
Sff . . .	Sforzandissimo.
Sin'. . . .	Sino.
Smorz. . .	Smorzando.
Sord. . . .	Sordini.
Sost. }	
Sosten. }	Sostenuto.
Stacc. . . .	Staccato.
String. . . .	Stringendo.
Sym. . . .	Symphony.
2ᵈᵃ. 2ᵈᵒ. .	Seconda. Secondo.

Saltando . .	[It.]	By skips.
Saltarello . .	[It.]	A very spirited Neapolitan dance in ⁴⁄₄ measure, very similar to the Italian tarentella.
Salto . . .	[It.]	A skip.
Sanft . . .	[G.]	Soft.
Sarabanda . .	[It.]	An antique slow dance tune.
Sartarello		(See Saltarello.)
Scherzandissimo	[It.]	Extremely light, playful, and quick.
Scherzando . .	[It.]	Light, playful, and quick.
Scherzo . .	[It.]	Very light, playful, and quick. A very light, playful, and quick movement.
Scherzoso . .	[It.]	In a light, playful, and spirited style.
Schlummerlied	[G.]	Cradle song.
Schnell Waltzer	[G.]	Quick waltzes.
Schreibart . .	[G.]	Style.
Schwach . .	[G.]	Piano. Soft.
Sciolto . . .	[It.]	Spry. Light. Spirited. Lively.
Scozzese . . .	[It.]	Scotch style.
Sdrucciolato . .	[It.]	Gliding. Sliding the fingers along the keys or strings of an instrument.
Sec	[F.]	Snappish. To cut or snap a note or a chord. (See page 20.)
Secco . . .	[It.]	
Seconda }	[It.]	Second. The second time.
Secondo }		
Segno . . .	[It.]	Sign. (See Al Segno.)
Segue }	[It.]	Now follows, or As follows. Also used as: In like manner, or Similar.
Seguito }		
Semi . . .	[L.]	Half.
Semplice . .	[It.]	With simplicity.
Semplicemente	[It.]	Simply.
Sempre. . .	[It.]	Always.
Sentimento }	[It.]	Feelingly, with expression.
Sentimentale }		
Sentita }	[It.]	Indicates to give the expression and accent, which the meaning of the music requires so that it may be well understood.
Sentito }		
Senza . . .	[It.]	Without.
Septet . . .	[It.]	A composition for seven instruments or voices.
Septetto . .		
Septuor . . .		
Sequence		A series of similar chords or intervals, etc.
Sequente . .	[It.]	Following. A succession.
Serenade . .	[F.]	A musical performance under the windows of the person to whom the honor is paid, generally late in the evening or at night. Also a musical composition consisting of song, recitative, and chorus; or any light
Serenata . .	[It.]	

		and pleasing instrumental composition consisting of several movements.
Seria . . .	[It.]	Serious. Tragic.
Serioso . . .	[It.]	Serious. Grave.
Serpeggiando.	[It.]	Gently creeping onwards.
Sestet . . .	[It.]	A composition for six voices or instruments.
Sestetto . .		
Sextu r		
Sforzandissimo	[It.]	With extreme force and emphasis.
Sforzando }	[It.]	With very much force and emphasis.
Sforzato }		
Siciliana . .	[It.]	A movement of a slow, soothing, pastoral character in ⁶⁄₈ measure, resembling the dance peculiar to the peasantry of Sicily.
Siegue		(See Segue.)
Silence		Remain silent. Wait a moment before playing.
Simile . . .	[It.]	As previously written. In like manner. Similarly.
Simili . . .	[L.]	
Simplice . .	[It.]	(See Semplice.)
Singhiozzando	[It.]	Sobbingly.
Sinistra . .	[It.]	The left hand.
Sinistro . .	[It.]	Dark and sad.
Sino. . . .	[It.]	As far as. To the.
Si Replica . .	[It.]	Repeat.
Si Tace . .	[It.]	Be silent. Do not play.
Slentando . .	[It.]	Diminish the movement gradually.
Slur		A curved line. (See pages 19 and 20; also "Note Tied" page 35 "Triplet" page 42, and Rule "Fifth" page 60.)
Smanioso . .	[It.]	Frantic. Furious; also, Enticing, Attractive.
Smorfioso . .	[It.]	With affectation.
Smorzando .	[It.]	Diminish the tone gradually.
Soave . . .	[It.]	Sweet and gentle.
Sòggetto . .	[It.]	Subject, melody, or theme.
Soli	[It.]	Implies that two or more principal parts play or sing together.
Solo	[It]	A composition or even a passage for a single voice or instrument. with or without accompaniment.
Sonata . . .	[It.]	A composition consisting of several movements, such as: an Allegro, an Andante, or Adagio; a Minuet and Trio, or Scherzo and Finale; generally for a single instrument, with or without accompaniment.
Sonate . . .	[F.]	
Sonatina . .	[It.]	A short and easy sonata.
Sonatine . .	[F.]	
Sonore . . .	[F.]	Sonorous. Full toned.
Sonoro . . .	[It.]	
Sopra . . .	[It.]	Above. Upper. Before.
Soprano . .	[It.]	The highest species of female voice.
Sordamente .	[It.]	Muffled. In an under tone. Use the damper pedal, (soft pedal.)
Sordini . . .	[It.]	Mutes or Dampers.
Sordino . .	[It.]	A mute or a damper applied to the bridge of the violin, etc.
Sospirando .	[It.]	With desire and apprehension.
Sostenuto . .	[It.]	Sustained. Continuous.
Sotto . . .	[It.]	Below. Under.
Sotto voce. .	[It.]	In a soft and subdued tone.
Sound		(See page 10.) One sound differs from another by its "timbre," its "intensity," and its "intonation." The timbre of a sound is the quality of its tone. For instance, a bell has more or less silver in its com-

position, and its timbre changes accordingly; the sound of a voice can easily be distinguished from that of a trumpet or of a violin, because the timbre is different.

The intensity of a sound is its greater or lesser power or volume.

The intonation of a sound is its pitch.

Spianato	[It.]	Even. Smooth. Tranquil.
Spiccato	[It.]	Very clear and distinct.
Spirito	[It.]	Spirited.
Spiritoso	[It.]	Very spirited.
Sta ⎱ Stat ⎰	[It.]	As it stands.
Staccatissimo	[It.]	Full staccato. (See page 19.)
Staccato	[It.]	(See page 19.)
Stark	[G.]	Forte, loud.
Stentato	[It.]	Over-loud.
Stesso	[It.]	The same.
Stibacchiato ⎱ Straccinato ⎰	[It.]	Dragging. Relaxing the movement or tempo.
Strain		A portion of a movement, generally divided off by a double bar.
Strascinato	[It.]	Dragging. Relaxing the movement or tempo.
Strathspey		A lively Scotch dance in Common time.
Streng	[G.]	Strict, in relation to style. Severe.
Strepito ⎱ Strepitoso ⎰	[It.]	In an impetuous style.
Stretto	[It.]	(See page 14.) In modern music, it implies an acceleration of time near the close of the piece.
Stricciando	[It.]	Dragging. Relaxing the movement or tempo.
String		Short or long wire used in musical instruments.
Stringendo	[It.]	Accelerating. Hurrying the movement or tempo.
Stück	[G.]	Piece.
Sub	[L.]	Below. Under.
Sub-dominant		(See page 50.)
Subito	[It.]	Sudden. Unexpected.
Super	[L.]	Above. Over.
Suspension		Implies that in the succession of two chords, one of the notes of the first chord is held through the second as an accidental note, although it occupies the place of a real note of the second chord on which it has its resolution. (Such an accidental note is an harmonic accidental note, because it belongs to the chord; while melodic ornaments are melodic accidental notes, because they do not belong to the chord.)
Sussurando	[It.]	Murmuringly. Warbling.
Symphony		(See page 15.)
Syncopation		(See page 59.)

ABBREVIATIONS.

T. S.	Tasto Solo.
Tem. ⎱ Temp. ⎰	Tempo.
Ten.	Tenuto.
Timp.	Timpani.
Tr.	Trill.
Tromb.	Tromba.

Tacet	[L.]	Silent. Implies that during a movement or part of a movement some particular instrument is to be silent.
Tanto	[It.]	Not so much. Not too much.
Tanz	[G.]	Danse.
Tänze	[G.]	Danses.
Tarantella	[It.]	A very spirited Italian dance in ⅜ measure, supposed to have the virtue of curing the bite of a venomous species of spider, called "Tarantella;" from which it takes its name.
Tardano		(See Ritardando.)
Tarentelle	[F.]	(See Tarantella.)
Tasto Solo	[It.]	Indicates that certain bass notes are not to be accompanied by chords in the right hand.
Tedesca ⎱ Tedesco ⎰	[It.]	In the German style.
Tema	[It.]	Theme. Melody. Air.
Tempestoso	[It.]	Violently agitated. Tempestuous.
Tempo	[It.]	Tempo or movement. In time. (See A tempo.)
Teneramente	[It.]	Tenderly. Affectionately.
Tenerezza	[It.]	Affection. Love.
Tenero	[It.]	Affectionate.
Tenuto ⎱ Tenute ⎰	[It.]	Implies that a note or notes must be held on, sustained. Also, to be very exact to hold some particular note or notes the whole of their value.
Ter	[It.]	Thrice.
Terzetto	[It.]	A short trio.
Theme		Theme. Subject. Melody. Air.
Thorough-bass		(See page 14.)
Timbre		(See "Sound" in Musical Dictionary.)
Timorosamente	[It.]	Timidly.
Timorosita	[It.]	Timidity.
Timoroso	[It.]	Timid.
Timpani		(See page 12.)
Tiranna	[It.]	A Spanish national air.
Toccata	[It.]	A solo of very difficult execution, generally for the organ or piano.
Toccatina	[It.]	A short toccata.
Tone		(See page 37; also, "Sound" in Musical Dictionary.)
Tonic ⎱ Tonique ⎰	[F.]	Key-note. (See page 50.)
Tosto	[It.]	Quick. Prompt.
Tradotto	[It.]	Arranged. Adapted.
Tranquillamente	[It.]	Tranquilly. Composedly.
Tranquillezza	[It.]	Tranquillity.
Tranquillo	[It.]	Tranquil.
Tre	[It.]	Three.
Tre corde	[It.]	Indicates to leave the damper (soft) pedal. (See page 25; also, "Una Corda" in Musical Dictionary.)
Tremando	[It.]	(See Tremolando, etc.)
Tremendo	[It.]	Terrible. Fearful.
Tremolando ⎱ Tremolate ⎱ Tremolo ⎰	[It.]	Implies the reiteration of a note or chord with great rapidity, so as to produce a tremulous kind of motion.
Triad		A chord of three notes. (See "Perfect chord, page 52.)
Trillando	[It.]	A succession of trills on different notes. (See "Trill," pages 76 and 77.)
Trill		(See pages 76 and 77.)
Trinkleid	[G.]	A drinking song.
Trio	[It.]	A composition for three voices or instruments. This term also denotes a second movement to a waltz, march,

		minuet, etc., which always leads back to a repetition of the first or principal movement.
Triplet		A group of three notes arising from the division of a note into three equal parts of the next inferior duration. (See page 42.)
Trochee		A dissyllabic foot composed of one long and one short syllable.
Tromba . .	[It.]	A trumpet. (See Trumpet, page 12.)
Trombone . .	[It.]	(See page 12.)
Troppo . . .	[It.]	Too much.
Trugschluss .	[G.]	An interrupted cadence.
Trumpet . . .		(See page 12.)
Tutta forza .	[It.]	With all possible power.
Tutte corde .	[It.]	Upon all the strings. Indicates to leave the damper (soft) pedal. (See Tre Corde.)
Tutti . . .	[It.]	All. A term pointing out those passages where all the voices or instruments, or both, perform together.
Tyrolienne .	[F.]	A song or dance peculiar to the inhabitants of the Tyrol. Very attractive by its simplicity and rhythm.

ABBREVIATION.

Unis . .		Unisoni.

Ubung . . .	[G.]	A study or exercise.
Ugualmente .	[It.]	All alike.
Un	[It.]	A, as: Un poco, a little.
Und	[G.]	And.
Una Corda .	[It.]	(See page 25.) Upon only one string, press down the damper (soft) pedal. When the damper pedal (soft pedal) is pressed down, the key-board of a grand piano moves to the right, thus the hammers strike only one string. When the damper pedal should be left it is expressed by "tre corde," (that is, three strings,) because by leaving it, the key-board returns to its proper place and naturally the hammers strike the usual number of strings. (See "Piano," also "Pedal," in Musical Dictionary.)
Unison		Perfect identity in pitch of two or more notes. (See "Remark," page 53.)
Unisoni } Unisono }	[It.]	This term implies that two, three or more parts are to play in unison, or if this be not practicable at least in octaves.

ABBREVIATIONS.

V.		Violin.
Var. . . .		Variation.
Vᵃ.		Viola.
Viol . . .		Violin.
Viol. 1ᵐ . . .		First Violin.
Vᵒ		Violino.
Vᵘⁱ . }		
Vcello. }		Violoncello.
Violonc. }		
V. S. . . .		Volti Subito.
V. V. . . .		Violini.

Va	[It.]	Continue. Keep on.
Variamento .	[It.]	Variation. In a varied and free style of execution.
Variazioni .	[It.]	Variations upon an air or theme.
Veloce . . .	[It.]	Light. Rapid.
Velocissimo .	[It.]	Extremely fast. With the utmost rapidity.
Velocita . .	[It.]	Rapidity. Velocity.
Veneziana . .	[It.]	Venetian style.
Vibrante . .	[It.]	A peculiar manner of touching the keys of the piano, which gives a full, vibrating, and thrilling tone.
Vibrate. . .	[It.]	Vibrating tone.
Vibratissimo .	[It.]	In an extreme vibrating tone.
Vibrato . .	[It.]	(See Vibrate.)
Vigore . . .	[It.]	Vigor.
Vigorosamente	[It.]	Vigorously. Firmly.
Vigoroso . .	[It.]	Vigorous.
Viola } Viole }	[It.]	(See Viola, page 12.)
Viol di Gamba	[It.]	An instrument resembling the violoncello, but having six strings.
Violin } Violino } . .	[It.]	(See Violin, page 12.)
Violini . . .	[It.]	Violins.
Violoncello .	[It.]	(See page 12.)
Violoncelli .	[It.]	Violoncellos.
Violone } Violono }	[It.]	Double-bass. (See Double-bass, page 12.)
Vistamente .	[It.]	Promptly. Quickly.
Vivace . . .	[It.]	Quick. Very quick.
Vivacissimo .	[It.]	Extremely quick.
Vivacita . .	[It.]	Quickness. Vivacity.
Vivamente. .	[It.]	Quickly.
Vivezza . .	[It.]	Vivacity. Vigor. Efficiency.
Vivo . . .	[It.]	Spirited. Lively. With fire.
Vocalize . .	[It.]	To practise singing on the Italian vowel A.
Voce . . .	[It.]	Voice. Also used to express "tone." (See Sotto voce.)
Volante. . .	[It.]	Light and rapid. With extreme swiftness.
Volata . . .	[It.]	A rapid succession of notes.
Voll . . .	[G.]	Full. Complete.
Vollkommen .	[G.]	Perfect.
Volta . . .	[It.]	Time, as : Prima Volta, first time.
Volti Subito .	[It.]	Turn over suddenly and quickly.

Walzer. . .	[G.]	A waltz.
Wechselnoten	[G.]	Melodic ornaments.
Weiche . . .	[G.]	Minor.
Wesentlich .	[G.]	Essential.
Wiederholung	[G.]	Repetition.
Wiedersehen .	[G.]	Return.

Zampogno .	[It.]	In the style of the bagpipe.
Zart . . .	[G.]	Soft. Tender.
Zeitmass . .	[G.]	Movement or Tempo.
Zelo . . .	[It.]	Zeal.
Zeloso . . .	[It.]	Zealous. With zeal.
Zerstreut . .	[G.]	Dispersed.
Zingaresca .	[It.]	Gypsy style.
Zoppa } Zoppo } . .	[It.]	Constrained. In a limping manner. A style of melody in which a long note is placed between two short notes.